# OVERTHINKING:

## HOW TO DECLUTTER YOUR MIND, IMPROVE YOUR SELF-CONFIDENCE AND MANAGE NEGATIVE THOUGHTS. REWIRE YOUR BRAIN, CURE ANXIETY AND RELIEVE STRESS USING SUCCESS HABITS & MINDFULNESS EXERCISES

**By Stephen Cure**

# Table of Contents

# Introduction

Overthinking is a critical and global issue that has affected millions of people. Many people do know what it is on the surface, but don't have an in-depth knowledge of how it invigorates our minds. Most people living in the world do not have an idea that they are overthinkers. Overthinking is not a disease, but an unhealthy habit that leads us to no good. It's more dangerous and potent than nuclear weapons.

So how do you know that you overthink issues? How do you know that you are not overthinking? How do you know that your mind is healthy and that you are not suffering from any overthinking related problems? What causes overthinking? How can overthinking be curtailed? Does it have any psychological, emotional, or physical effect on the affected victim? These and many more are what this book is trying to expound.

In addition to overthinking, this book is also addressing how important it is to maintain a positive mindset, not just in a work or school setting, but in every place that you go to and maintaining it all the time. The issue of clutter is again, another global problem that affects people's productivity and concentration levels. At a workplace, school, industrial sites, retail businesses, having a cluttered mind results in zero progress. A cluttered mind is blocking yourself from seeing opportunities and acknowledging them. This book critically explained what these clutters are, why they are present, who gets them, it's the effect and possible solutions on how to stop them. One of the solutions, as explained in detail in this book to stop your mind from being cluttered is by thinking positively. We explained how this curtail a cluttered mind, alongside other useful solutions, provided in this book.

The people you associate with also influence you. Associating with the negative ones will derail you from achieving your goals and becoming productive. Maintaining a positive circle, on the other hand is advantageous and by far, what you need to be progressive. This book discussed tips on how to overcome these negative people and how to attract positivity into your life.

Many people are unaware that the environment has a psychological effect on a person. How cluttered an environment is determines your level of work input and output. This book talked about the psychological effects these clutter have on a person and ways to declutter an environment for maximum output. This book provides all the useful information you need to declutter your mind and set it free from the clutches of overthinking. With practical tips enumerated and explained in this book, you, as the reader is sure of having a positive impact after reading.

# Chapter 1  : Thoughts

Let's talk about what it is and what aspects the discipline of the psychology of thought addresses. First, I will define some terms that will be necessary to understand this discipline. I am going to explain them in the order in which they are involved in the process of "thinking":

**Perception:** captures what happens in the environment, figures and shapes are identified as human beings and characteristics of the environment, what is observed is fitted with what was expected to be observed in a family situation?

Attention: begin to actively capture what is happening.

**Thinking:** The cognitive process of thinking involves what has just happened, using prior knowledge and a general understanding of the situation.

**Memory:** the knowledge that we have about what has happened and the interpretations that have been made are stored.

**Language:** search for words that best express thoughts and choose the ones that you think will best evoke in other people the situation as it has been lived.

## What is the activity of thinking?

Cognition is the set of activities for which information is processed by the psychic apparatus: reception, selection, organization, transformation and elaboration. It is based on the activity of the subject, who receives information from both the physical and social environment, to understand it, representing reality and giving it meaning.

## What psychological processes are involved?

Knowledge includes cognitive processes (perception, attention, memory, language and thought) and motivational and emotional processes. Cognitive processes comprise the representation of images, diagrams, concepts and categories; deductive or inductive reasoning; and problem solving, through information processing, creativity and decision making.

## What is thought?

There is difficulty in defining this concept due to the breadth of said concept, the multiple activities involved in said process, and the various factors involved such as the subject, the activity, the content, the verbal expression and the object.

Thought integrates behavior as one of its phases. It is the cognitive process that generates probable behavioral predictions, that is, the thought we have in the face of a situation probably marks how we will act.

It is a directed and cognitive process, with a sequential and complex nature. It is a high cognitive level process, in which other cognitive processes are also involved.

Comprehension intervenes in thought with the functions of representing and organizing knowledge and interpreting and generating inferences.

# Chapter 2 : Decluttering Your Mind

You must learn to declutter your mind, removing all of your unnecessary thoughts to make room for the most important thoughts. Practicing minimalism in your life can help you to focus on what matters the most to you and what it is that you truly value in life. You must, of course, learn how to focus. There are a few ways to do this and make it easier for yourself to focus your attention properly. Finally, you can make focusing easier by prioritizing your tasks. Determine what you want to focus on, and put it in writing so that you have a visual representation of your most important tasks. By doing so, you will be able to start focusing and stop being so overwhelmed by all of your thoughts.

You must declutter your mind; it is essential to your mental health, productivity, and ability to concentrate. If you have a cluttered mind, you may struggle to sleep at night. You won't be able to focus on work. It will be difficult to enjoy your life when you are weighed down with countless thoughts and filled with worries. There are a few ways that you can work on decluttering your mind.

One way to declutter your mind is to declutter your physical space. You may be mentally overwhelmed because of the physical environment that you are in. If your workspace is unorganized and filled with junk, your mind will reflect that; you won't be able to focus on your work. For this reason, it's necessary to go through your space and get rid of anything that you don't need. This will allow you to focus on what's important. Your home, workspace, and car will all influence your mental health. Put yourself in an environment that helps you to focus instead of distracting you from focusing.

Another way to declutter your mind is learning how to not multi-task. It is instinctual to multi-task, as it seems like a way of getting more done. However, you are splitting your focus among several tasks instead of giving your total focus to one. This will result in work that is of a lower quality, and you will feel overwhelmed as a result. Start making it a habit to completely finish one task before moving onto another. You will notice a dramatic change for doing so, as you will accomplish more and feel better about your work.

Be decisive. Instead of putting tasks off until later, decide what to do at the moment. If you have an important task that will take less than five minutes to accomplish, get it done first. Overthinking frequently occurs as a result of a potential decision; you don't want to make the wrong choice. If you struggle with making a decision, jot down all of the potential pros and cons of making each choice. Use that to guide you in the decision-making process. You will receive the opportunity to make more decisions each day. If you let those collect by constantly putting them off until later,you will inevitably reach a point where you feel extremely overwhelmed. Decide what to do with the tasks that matter and eliminate those that don't. For decisions you must make, get it over with instead of procrastinating.

You can also declutter the number of decisions that you must make. You may also prepare ahead of time so that you feel better when it happens. For instance, you may plan your outfits for the entire week on Sunday night. You may meal-prep so that you don't have to worry about food when it's mealtime. Make a schedule for routine tasks you must complete, such as doing laundry every Thursday morning or vacuuming every Wednesday night. Reducing your decisions and coming up with a schedule can help you to stop overthinking and have a schedule that you already know works for you. You may make a schedule for yourself so that you know exactly what to do.

| Sunday | Monday | Tuesday | Wednesday | Thursday | Friday | Saturday |
|---|---|---|---|---|---|---|
| Pick clothes | Bathroom | Dishes | Vacuum | Laundry | Trash | Meal-prep |

## Minimalism

Minimalism, typically regarded as an intense trend, is quite helpful for those who wish to focus more clearly. Although some take this to the extreme and live out of a suitcase and choose to not have a home or car, minimalism is a practice of being more mindful of what you choose to keep in your life. It can be applied across your life to help you to only have what matters to you in your life. You may find yourself practicing minimalism in one area of your life, only to have that affect other areas of your life.

Minimalism isn't simply getting rid of things or decluttering your belongings. It is seeing what truly matters to you and sticking with that. Marie Kondo's method is to only keep items that "spark joy." This means that you only keep the items in your life that truly make you happy. It can help you to go through each item that you own and decide what matters to you. You may have some things that you keep out of guilt or for "someday in the future." However, these items will only disappoint and frustrate you each time you see them. It is important to eliminate any items that bring you negativity or remind you of failure. Surround yourself with items that bring you joy and make you a better person. Your surroundings should be a reflection of you and what you love. You may choose to go through the items in your house, at work, in your car, and any other places that you may have. Do not bring any other items into your life that bring you down in any way; only own what you truly need to make you happy. This can help you to have a much clearer mind.

Additionally, you may practice digital minimalism. You may feel overwhelmed with the amount of information that you have coming in. There will constantly be e-mails, texts, and other notifications. Social media can also be quite overwhelming. Delete any apps that you don't use or that you don't find happiness from. Get rid of that educational app that you "should" be using but never do. Get rid of those storage-sucking apps that you don't like. Clean up your phone. Turn off notifications that you don't need. You may go through your e-mails and delete all the ones you don't need. Unsubscribe from e-mails. Create a labeling system. For social media, unfollow those who don't have a positive effect on your life. You may even choose to stop using social media or go on a social media detox. Limit yourself to a certain amount of time for social media. There is so much information that comes from social media, and much of it is unnecessary. Make sure that you are spending your time the way you want to be spending it.

**Learning to Focus**

Take some time to reflect on where you stand with your focus. Are you happy with your ability to focus? Do you wish that your focus could be improved? Figure out what your goal is. Do you find yourself getting distracted easily, unable to continue work after taking a break, or simply can't finish tasks with ease? Determine what it is that prevents you from focusing.

You may try to challenge yourself. Give yourself a task and a time limit and do your best. Become aware of how often you become distracted and how easily you can regain your focus. Write down anything that distracts you; you may not even realize how distracted you become! Afterward, ensure that you rid yourself of any distractions. Turn off your notifications. Make sure that it's quiet and peaceful. Whatever distracts you, make sure it's eliminated. You may also come up with a schedule for your breaks. Figure out what works best for you. Perhaps you like to work for fifty minutes and take a ten-minute break. Perhaps you prefer to work longer and have a longer break. It will depend on your personal preference. Regardless, it's important to remain completely focused while you are working and to also take breaks regularly. This will increase your productivity and allow you to be less stressed. Determine what sets you off. What is it that makes you lose your focus? Why do you overthink? Reflecting can help you to determine the causes of your actions.

There are a few ways that you may work on your focus. Meditating can help you to be calm and live in the moment. You will learn how to become a master of your mind. This can help if you feel overwhelmed by your thoughts. Although meditation can seem difficult (and even frustrating) at first, it provides you with a great boost to your mental health, ability to concentrate, and overall emotional well-being. Another way to help you to focus is by doing some physical activity. Taking a quick walk can help to get your blood flowing, ease up the tension, and wake you up. It can be quite refreshing to get moving, even if you simply take a moment to stretch. Remaining active can also help improve your physical health, which affects your mental health. This is why keeping your physical health in check is so important. Getting the proper amount of sleep, consuming the right foods, and drinking enough water every day is crucial. You will not only feel better, but you will also be able to focus much better.

Overall, it's important to take care of your mental health so that you can focus better. By taking some time to yourself and doing small things that you love, you can help yourself to feel better. When you are happy, you will feel much more motivated and find it much easier to focus.

## Prioritizing

Perhaps you are able to focus, but you simply aren't focusing on what you should. It can be quite easy to get caught up in tasks that are unimportant or aren't urgent. You may think that you're being productive, but you're procrastinating. This is why prioritizing is so important. You must be able to recognize where you should be placing your focus. Otherwise, it's like you're on a treadmill. You're still getting something done, but you aren't going anywhere. You must learn to prioritize your tasks properly so that you focus first on what's important. After that, you may move on to other tasks.

One way to prioritize is by making to-do lists every day. It is helpful to make them the night before so that you can plan ahead of time. At the moment, you may not feel as motivated to accomplish every task. It helps to have one to three major tasks for the day. These are your top tasks. Even if they are the only things you accomplish for the day, you would be happy with yourself. These are your top priority, and it is what you should focus on accomplishing first. This will allow you to focus on what you must.

You should also write down any additional goals that you have for the day. Write every possible thing that is on your mind. Make a list of all of the potential tasks, even if they aren't necessary for the day. By doing a "brain dump," you are freeing yourself of clutter in your mind. This will help you to focus on the present instead of the past or future. Additionally, you will feel better knowing that you won't forget anything that you would like to do. It will all be written down, so you can feel more at peace.

**Brain Dump**

Need to do progress towards completing a project, go grocery shopping, go to the bank, clean kitchen, take the dog to the groomer, do laundry and wash sheets, go to the gym, talk to sister about dinner, schedule dentist appointment, etc.

You may also consider journaling to help you figure out what matters. Each day, you may reflect on your day. Determine what your strengths and weaknesses for that day were. How was your focus? Did you accomplish everything? This will also help you to determine how you can improve for the next day. Although it will take time to become better at focusing, you may practice and improve your skills every day. Eventually, you will naturally prioritize your tasks and focus. Until then, you must make a conscious effort to do so.

Prioritizing your tasks will allow you to accomplish what is urgent and important first. Tasks with deadlines or of greater importance will be completed first. By doing this, you are allowing yourself to not feel guilty, as you will complete what you must before moving onto less urgent and less important activities. You can even reward yourself with some fun after completing your daily tasks. When you procrastinate, you are clouding your focus and delaying the completion of important tasks. You are hindering your performance and missing out on opportunities. When you learn how to focus, you will feel much better and will reduce your overthinking tendencies.

It's very important to learn how to focus. You are likely overwhelmed with all of the information that you receive, all of the tasks that you must complete, and all of the thoughts in your head. Each day brings new surprises and new information with it. It's important to be able to have a filter on it to allow yourself to focus on what you must. Otherwise, you will constantly feel anxious, stress, and overwhelmed by all of the thoughts in your head. This will lead to overthinking, as you will think about the potential tasks to complete and won't have a plan for it. As a result, you won't be able to enjoy the present moment because you are so focused on your past failures and worried about making future mistakes. However, learning to focus can help you.

Decluttering your mind will help you to remove all of your unnecessary thoughts. You will learn how to focus on what matters so that you may direct your energy towards that. Similarly, practicing minimalism will help you to understand what you value in life. You will realize what you should put your focus on, and what you find important. You can learn to focus on utilizing a few methods. Physical and mental health will play a huge role in your ability to focus. Finally, prioritizing will help you to learn what you should focus your attention on. You will feel more at ease when you can focus on what you need to.

# Chapter 3  : Causes of Overthinking

There is a high possibility of experiencing somatopsychological problems if your vagus nerve is inflamed or damaged. These problems are mostly related to your psychological aspect and can only be noticed through your actions, and they initiated in your head as it depends on how your brain responds to different situations, so you need to understand the two systems of the vagus nerve continuously communicate with the brain, mainly about other body organs. The sympathetic nervous system is responsible for keeping you in action by feeding the cortisol and the adrenaline while the parasympathetic nervous system is reliable while you are relaxed or resting.

In other words, the sympathetic system activates actions while the parasympathetic decelerates actions and keeps you at rest. However, the latter utilizes acetylcholine as neurotransmitters that control the blood pressure and the heart rate to create a perfect condition for relaxation. As a part of the body's autonomous nervous system, the vagus nerve may fail or experience damage hindering its full potential to the body. The most common condition that affects the vagal nerve is inflammation that makes it malfunction. This condition could worsen the functioning of the whole body as the vagal nerve facilitates essential processes that keep the body healthy and kicking.

## Chronic stress

The problem is associated with overthinking things that might be beyond your control. Stress can also be a result of issues in your vagal nerve. For instance, when your body is exposed to harmful situations, it releases chemicals that are meant to respond appropriately and avoid injury. As noted before, the sympathetic nervous system stimulates the response through the fight-or-flight reaction, and it is at this time that your heart rate increases to quickly supply blood to the rushing body parts and muscles. The response likewise enhances the quickened inhalation of oxygen to assist in blood oxygenation. In this case, stress acts as a protective mechanism that your body initiates to keep you alert and out of danger.

There are different perceptions of stress among people. In other words, what causes stress for one person might be of little concern to the other, and people have different ways and potential to deal with it. This means that if stress is meant to prevent you from danger, then it should not be treated as a bad thing. Besides, our bodies have a unique mechanism that is intended to deal with specific doses of stress. However, the body's capabilities could weaken as you may be overwhelmed by chronic stress that could be as a result of vagal nerve inflammation or damage. This type of stress impacts almost every aspect of your life, including physical health and emotions. Chronic stress is also characterized by low esteem where you feel worthless and not comfortable while in public.

If you are suffering from chronic stress, you are likely to feel overwhelmed and easily agitated by others. As a result, you end up avoiding interactions with your peers as you feel they want to control you. Avoiding people and having low self-esteem makes you suffer in isolation as you may not realize the seriousness of the condition. With this in mind, the emotional symptoms of chronic stress could end up being a serious condition if not detected and treated. Consequently, your judgment becomes impaired by the condition as you get prone to the inability to focus and forgetfulness. You also remain pessimistic and unable to view your life positively and exhibit nervousness through behaviors such as fidgeting and nail-biting.

First, people with chronic stress seem to avoid complex responsibilities. They also experience sudden changes in your appetite where they either eat excessively or not eat at all. Second, procrastination is also associated with chronic stress, and you could be at risk of indulging in alcohol and drug abuse. Therefore, you should ask for feedback if you think that you are suffering from stress. A doctor will usually record the observations and what you report to come to a proper conclusion about the condition you are suffering from. In this case, the underlying cause of chronic stress is a dysfunctional vagus nerve, so you should take the necessary measures to ensure that you start vagal verve treatment to normalize its functionality.

## Anxiety and Panic Attacks

Whenever you come across a stressful situation, the body activates the sympathetic nervous system of the vagus nerve. In most cases, the system is reversed once the situation is over. However, the persistence of the tension would mean that the sensitive effect of the vagus nerve would be prolonged until you are out of harm's way. The effect is usually triggered and ended by a physiological response in your body, but a prolonged fight-or-flight response would cause problems for your body. The situation would lead to the activation of the intestine and the adrenal axis of the brain. As a result, the brain increases the production of hormones that travel through the bloodstream to stimulate the adrenaline and cortisol induction.

The hormones act as inflammatory precursors and immune suppressors, causing the anxiety that could make you ill and depressed, so the chronic anxiety increases the production of glutamate in the brain, which, when combined with cortisol, reduces the hippocampus in charge of memory retention. The worsening of this situation leads to the development of anxiety disorder characterized by panic attacks. The problem is characterized by a sense that you are in an impending danger or your life is at risk. These false signs may be frequent, depending on the seriousness of the condition. With this condition, you feel afraid of losing your valuables or as if you are about to die. In most cases, the effect seems uncontrollable as the panic creates an illusion that it has been decided elsewhere.

At this time, your heart rate is increased due to the tension, making it pound on your chest as your breath goes wild. The blood pressure increases as the body take it as an attack. These panic attacks might confuse your body as they give false alarms making your body sweat as if you are in a serious situation even though you may be lying on your couch. The helplessness associated with anxiety and panic attacks leaves you trembling with fear of imagined imminent danger, and you will realize that your body is shaking uncontrollably due to a perceived situation.

The quickened breathing associated with anxiety makes your throat experience fast air movement as the lungs try to suck as much air as possible to supply to the heart, resulting to experience tightness in your throat and a burning effect. You may also fall short of breath as the heart rate increases, as well as experience prolonged chills if you suffer from anxiety and panic attacks. These chills could be against the sweating and heat produced by the body as your adrenaline keeps you in the fight-or-flight reaction. This problem makes you look confused and unaware of the immediate environment.

The condition should be taken seriously as it could lead to suicidal thoughts and actions as the victim sees no other way out. This is because the experiences in the body are severe and complicated and would require immediate treatment to avoid causing accidents and incidents. The hot rashes experienced in this problem are experienced in the neck, chest, or stomach and are indications that the body is at the full alert of the faced danger. Generally, these illusions make the person feel detached from the real world and it would be hard to communicate with them when under panic attacks. In other words, their mind takes them to the world where they see a danger in every corner. The total panic is so real that the person continually experiences a tingling and numb sensation.

Other characteristics of anxiety and panic attacks include headache, chest pain, and dizziness, especially after the attack is over. During this time, the victim relaxes and tries to recover lost energy, but with chronic panic attacks, the victim keeps on worrying that the experience may happen again. They also feel uncomfortable associating with others and attending public functions as they are wary of possible attacks. At this time, the body exerts these symptoms due to the confusion caused by the dysfunctional vagus nerve, so if you experience these symptoms, you should see a doctor check on the condition of your vagus nerve and take the necessary measures.

## Phobias

Vagal inflammation is known to cause phobias as one of the somatopsychological problems in the human body. Mostly, the problem is characterized by a deep sense of panic and irrational fear reaction. When you are in this condition, you encounter different sources of fear, depending on how you perceive the environment. In some instances, you could be experiencing phobia in specific situations, objects, or places. This form of vagal nerve damage is known to complicate how your brain interprets some aspects of the environment, so you end up feeling insecure in dark or quiet environments, especially if you have had a frightening experience before.

The effects of phobia vary depending on the seriousness as well as the body's mechanism to repair damaged tissues. These conditions determine the impact of phobia in your body as it could only be an annoying experience or build up to a severe and disabling. If you experience phobia, you might be helpless about it as it is caused by other underlying conditions such as vagal nerve inflammation. Therefore, you are prone to stress as you always remain afraid of a possible attack, making you unproductive and unsocial, especially in the workplace. The condition may be different from one person to the other, hence the different categorization according to the trigger and symptoms.

One common type of the condition is known as agoraphobia which is characterized by the panic of situations and places that you cannot escape from. Mostly, people who have agoraphobia are afraid of being in open places such as outside their houses or in crowded places. People feel uncomfortable while in social areas and like to stay most of their time indoors. The main reason why these people avoid public places is due to the anxiety of experiencing phobia publicly, which might embarrass them and leave them helpless. In some cases, people with agoraphobia may experience a health emergency, making them remain in places where they could ask for an urgent response.

Social phobia has relatively similar characteristics and is also known as social anxiety disorder when combined with symptoms of anxiety. As the name suggests, the victims of this disorder avoid social places and prefer staying in isolation for fear of humiliation and discrimination in case they become phobic. This type of phobia is so serious as it could be caused by a simple interaction such as answering a phone call or talking to a stranger. It makes the victims go out of their way to avoid these interactions making life hard for them, especially if they are working or attending school. A phobia may be triggered by a specific object with common categories being the environment, medical, situations, or animals.

In this case, you experience phobia after experiencing environmental conditions such as storm or lightning, while an animal phobia is as a result of encountering animals such as rodents or snakes. In medical phobia, you feel threatened by the sight of blood or syringe. These experiences are hard to live with, and you should take the necessary steps to ensure that the condition is controlled to help you live happily and fearlessly. The problem is characterized by uncontrollable anxiety, especially when you experience a source of fear. Also, you may find yourself doing extra lengths to ensure that you avoid perceived sources of concern even if it means changing direction. If you are affected by this problem, you are likely to be unproductive in your workplace as you could not function properly when the source of fear is around.

It will be hard to control the feeling even after you realize that the fear is exaggerated, unreasonable, and irrational. Some of the physical effects of phobia include trembling and abnormal breathing. At this time, the body is accelerating the supply of blood and chemicals to the body to tackle the perceived threat, and there is confusion and disorientation as you remain stuck between understanding the danger and taking swift action to get out of danger. The accelerated heartbeats are likely to cause abnormal breathing which could lead to pain in the chest as the lungs try to grasp as much oxygen as they can. The best remedy for this condition would be to understand the underlying cause and seek medical help to repair and heal the damaged vagus nerve.

**Bipolar disorder**

The problem is also caused by vagal dysfunction and inflammation and was formerly referred to as manic depression. It is a mental condition that triggers a moody feeling and swinging emotions. When the emotions are high, they are referred to as mania or hypomania, and depression when they are low. If you are depressed, you probably will experience hopelessness, sadness, and lost pleasure and interest. The feeling makes you hate activities that you liked before and lose interest in meeting the people you love. However, the feeling is sometimes short-lived as you may suddenly experience high moods that make you feel euphoric and irritably full of energy.

The drastic changes in mood significantly affect how you behave, judge, or sleep. It also hinders you from clear reasoning and making the right decision. There are numerous episodes of these mood swings that occur several times annually. In some cases, you may experience changes in events and emotional symptoms, while others may not experience them at all. The condition is manageable through the follow up of a treatment plan that includes counseling and medication. When a dysfunctional vagus nerve causes the condition, it could only be treated by healing the nerve. Several types of this disorder include depression and hypomania. These symptoms could cause drastic life effects and significant distress if left unaddressed.

Bipolar disorder is experienced when the condition triggers a break from reality and makes you fear your imagination. It is characterized by a single manic episode and occurs either before or after the incident. Bipolar II is characterized by a major depressive episode that lasts for weeks followed by a hypomanic episode that happens for about a week. The condition is more common in women but is also experienced by men. In cyclothymia, you experience bouts of depression and hypomania, which are relatively shorter than those caused by the last two types. Additionally, the condition is characterized by a month or two for stability when the problem recurs and extends for some weeks. The mania and hypomania episodes are distinct in their symptoms, but the mania episode is more severe and is known to cause problems in public places such as workplaces or schools.

The condition also affects your relationship with your peers and family as it distances you from the reality hence the need to take drastic measures to curb it. The mania and hypomania episodes are characterized by jumpy and abnormal upbeats where you remain restless and agitated by things that might be perceived or out of control. The condition increases your activities as you seem to have extra energy to perform various tasks. These episodes make you feel overconfident and a sense of well-being, assuring you that you can succeed in everything you try and that you are perfect. The euphoria could lead to embarrassment as you try to prove your point. You run out of control in whatever you do as you seem to take over the management in your company or want to replace the monitor in your class.

You may always remain and uncontrollably talkative and seem excited about topics that could be boring to your audience. Bipolar disorder keeps your body engaged, hence the talkativeness and overreaction to minor things. Your thoughts also remain at a high rate as they think about things that could be out of the world. The increased interest in uncommon things could make you lose interest and easily diverted to other topics, so you quickly lose interest and remain unpredictable on the issues that you would address. The major depressive episodes cause noticeable difficulties in your daily activities with most of the symptoms being psychological. The effects could make you lose or gain weight as you suffer from swing appetite. The feeling of worthlessness associated with this disorder could lead to inappropriate guilt. If you suffer from this condition, you are likely to have difficulties thinking or concentrating with a high possibility of developing suicidal thoughts. For that reason, you should understand the underlying cause of the condition and take drastic measures to address it. With the healing of the vagal nerve, you are sure to regain your consciousness and suppress the disorder.

As you have probably already figured out, vagus nerve plays a really important role in our life in terms of psychological and physical wellness, and it is strictly correlated to the topic of this book. That's why I have preferred to give it the space it deserved, thus we will talk deeply about it at the end of the book.

# Chapter 4 : How to Identify If You Are an Overthinker

## Signs You Could Be an Overthinker

### When you talk fast

A person may appear to be nervous when they talk fast without pausing. However, this could be a sign that the person is an overthinker. A lot is usually happening inside an overthinker's mind. A person's mind may wander deep in thoughts, causing them to have a lot to say even though other people may not follow precisely what that person is talking about.

### When you find yourself comparing people

Sometimes overthinkers shift to a perfectionist mindset, and they start comparing other people and things to imagined standards of perfection. Such measures could come from Social Media and Media in general, where people make out everything to be perfect.

### You Overanalyze Everything

If you notice that you overanalyze everything around you, then you are certainly an overthinker. This means that you may try to find a deeper meaning in all the experiences that you go through. When meeting new people, instead of engaging in productive communication, you may focus instead on how other people perceive you. Someone could be giving you a particular look and you may make several assumptions just based on that look. Overthinking consumes you. You end up wasting a lot of energy trying to figure out and make sense of the world around you. What you don't realize is that not everything has intrinsic meaning.

## You Think Too Much but Don't Act

An overthinker will be affected by something called analysis paralysis. This is a scenario where you think too much about something but don't do anything about it in the end. In this case, you spend a lot of time weighing the options you have at your disposal. At first, you make up your mind on what the best alternative might be. Later, you compare your decision to other possible decisions that you could take. This means that you can't stop thinking about the possibilities and whether or not you made the right decision.

## You Can't Let Go

Often, we make erroneous decisions that could lead us to fail. When this happens, it can be daunting to let go more so when you reflect on the sacrifices you have made to get to the point you are at. You might feel that it is painful to let go after you have invested a lot of money on a certain business.

**You Always Want to Know Why**

Without a doubt, the notion of asking why can be helpful to solve problems. This is because this probing attitude gets you the answers that you might be looking for. Nonetheless, it can also be damaging when you can't help but always wonder why. Overthinkers maintain such investigative attitude throughout their lives.

**You Analyze People**

The way you see other people can also say a lot about you. In most cases, you get lost thinking too much about how other people behave. You may tend to judge everybody that you come across. This one walks funnily. That person is not dressed well. You wonder what someone sitting at the park is smiling about. When these thoughts fill your head, you will only drain yourself. Spending too much time focusing on other people will only deter you from using your mind productively. Instead of visualizing your goals and your future, you waste your energy mulling over little things that add no value to you.

**Regular Insomnia**

Do you find it hard to sleep sometimes? You may get worked up over the idea that your brain cannot shut down and stop thinking. Sadly, this can paralyze you since your brain doesn't get the rest that it deserves. Gradually, you will notice a decrease in your productivity. You are unlikely to feel good about yourself since there is little that you achieve. Worrying too much about not being able to sleep can make you uneasy and you may find yourself in a state of captivity.

## You Always Live in Fear

Are you afraid of what the future has in store for you? If you answer yes to this question, then chances are that you're caged in your mind. Living in fear could drive you to resort to drugs and alcohol as your best remedy. You will gain the perception that by taking drugs, it will help you drown your sorrows and help you forget.

## You're Always Fatigued

Do you always wake up in the morning feeling tired? This could be a result of stress or depression. Instead of living a productive life, you find yourself waking up late, tired, and unmotivated. This happens because you don't allow your mind to rest.

## You Don't Live in the Present

Do you find it difficult to enjoy life? Why do you think you find it daunting to sit back, relax, and be happy with your friends? The mere fact that you can't stay in the present implies that you won't focus on what is happening in the present. Overthinking blinds you from noticing anything good that is currently happening around you. You will often think about the worst that can happen. The issue is that you are trapped in your mind and there is nothing outside your thoughts that you can constructively think about.

## You crave for affection, yet don't always get it

Often, overthinking is just a ploy to get attention. While this isn't always the case, it might be worth asking yourself if it is just the comfort that you seek.

## You pay attention to others' assessments as well

Considering the opinions of others is crucial in understanding your feelings and what you can do about those issues which worry you.

## An overthinker attempts to locate importance in all things

Indeed, everything is urgent, everything is a life and death struggle, and everything is headed toward a tragic end.

## Experience the ill effects of sleep deprivation

It is common for overthinkers to lose sleep regularly. While it's normal when you have something important to worry about, the chronic overthinker will experience sleep deprivation issues as a result of their pathological worrying.

## Overthinkers recollect every word and detail from a discussion

If you find yourself keeping a play by play account of your conversations, then there is a very good chance you fall under the category of overthinkers.

## Overthinkers have trouble relating to others

These folks will find it hard to build lasting relationships especially if they are bent in seeing the worst of every situation.

## When your mood constantly changes

Overthinking causes hormonal imbalance in people, which is manifested by frequently occurring mood swings. Also, a person may experience anxiety, obsessive-compulsive disorder, addictions, and other mental health issues.

## When you notice weight variations

Overthinking causes stress, which leads to weight variations. It causes loss of appetite and loss of weight. Weight loss can happen over a few days, weeks, or even a few months. That is how the body responds to overthinking habits that increase metabolism. The body uses 'fuel' from the body's fat reserves when metabolism increases. In that way, a person experiences weight loss.

## When you are anxious and restless

Too much thinking leads to anxiety and restlessness, which, if not treated, become worse over time. When a person constantly thinks about finding a job, or feeling nervous before doing a big exam, or being embarrassed in particular social situations, her mind becomes restless, and even causes the person to develop fear.

## When you lack patience

A person will often feel impatient when they become too much engrossed in their thoughts. They may also become angry, irritated, and intolerant.

The body reacts to overthinking by releasing adrenaline or cortisol, which helps the body to respond to a stressful situation. For overthinkers, a stressful situation could be as small as someone else interrupting their thoughts. The overthinker will react in a way that could irritate another person.

## Things Overthinkers Do (That They Never Talk About)

If you are an overthinker, you limit your chances of becoming successful in life. It will prevent you from reaching your goals and make your life miserable.

## They apologize excessively

When you tell an overthinker that they have wronged you, before even identifying if the situation is their fault, they start to apologize. This leaves them exposed to additional criticism, which may or may not be warranted.

## Critical thinking is their thing

Most overthinkers are excellent critical thinkers. This is one of the excellent things about overthinking. An overthinker spends all of their time deliberating and analyzing each decision in an unending manner. Therefore, they often come up with the best results.

**They worry excessively about making others happy**

Overthinkers forget that they should be happy too. They worry about others' happiness, forgetting they need to be happy. They often negatively exaggerate how the world will view their feelings, actions, thoughts, decisions, and words.

This limits their progress and makes accomplishing their personal goals harder. They make decisions that please others, instead of themselves.

**Overthinkers may also be escape artists**

To escape their minds, overthinkers might resort to overworking, excessive activity, perfectionism, and other extreme habits to escape from their overthinking. Those with more serious issues may turn to state-altering medications or drugs to take the edge off.

**They experience severe headaches or migraines**

Catastrophic overthinking may cause somatization, such as headaches, stomachaches, etc. Those especially prone to worrying or overthinking may fear that their headache is a symptom of something more serious, which may make their headache even worse.

They research their purchases excessively or always need a second opinion

When making purchases, those that overthink may become paralyzed with the overabundance of options that are available to them. They may search online for hours for the best options. They may ask all of their friends' opinions.

## Their overthinking stems from insecurity

They often overthink because they are unsure of their decisions; this makes it hard for them to decide on what to do. At work, they might have issues choosing clients, projects, or the best course of action to take when problems arise. This lack of confidence can lead them to be doubted by others, even when they end up making the right decisions.

## They may become overly preoccupied

They may not be able to see the forest for the trees. When they become overly preoccupied, they may miss important dates or appointments.

# Chapter 5 : Overthinking and Mental / Behavioral Disorders

If you notice that you overanalyze everything around you, then you are certainly an overthinker. This means that you may try to find a deeper meaning in all the experiences that you go through. When meeting new people, instead of engaging in productive communication, you may focus instead on how other people perceive you. Someone could be giving you a particular look and you may make several assumptions just based on that look. Overthinking consumes you. You end up wasting a lot of energy trying to figure out and make sense of the world around you. What you don't realize is that not everything has intrinsic meaning.

## You Think Too Much, But Don't Act

An overthinker will be affected by something called analysis paralysis. This is a scenario where you think too much about something, but don't do anything about it in the end. In this case, you spend a lot of time weighing the options you have at your disposal. At first, you make up your mind on what the best alternative might be. Later, you compare your decision to other possible decisions that you could take. This means that you can't stop thinking about the possibilities and whether or not you made the right decision. Ultimately, you end up not making a decision. You only find yourself in a vicious circle where you simply think a lot, but there is little that you do. Perhaps the best strategy to prevent yourself from falling into a thinking trap is to try out the alternatives you have. A simple decision to act will make a huge difference.

## You Can't Let Go

Often, we make erroneous decisions that could lead us to fail. When this happens, it can be daunting to let go more so when you reflect on the sacrifices you have made to get to the point you are at. You might feel that it is painful to let go after you have invested a lot of money on a certain business. The issue here is that you don't want to fail. However, it is important to realize that failing to let go only holds you back from trying out something else that could work. It also affects your life since you will think repeatedly about your failures. You need to move on. You must shift your attention to something else instead of beating yourself up over something that is now out of your control. Convince yourself that there is nothing you can do about what has already happened apart from learning from it. The best thing you can do is to let go and move on.

## You Always Want to Know Why

Without a doubt, the notion of asking why can be helpful to solve problems. This is because this probing attitude gets you the answers that you might be looking for. Nonetheless, it can also be damaging when you can't help but always wonder why. Normally, we are accustomed to answering questions from kids. They just love to ask why about anything and everything. They will not hesitate to ask you why you don't talk to your neighbor. Why children are born or simply why you love to walk. There's something unique about how children are curious. Overthinkers maintain such investigative attitude throughout their lives. As adults, certain things only have surface meanings. Therefore, probing too much can only affect how other people see you.

## You Analyze People

The way you see other people can also say a lot about you. In most cases, you get lost thinking too much about how other people behave. You may tend to judge everybody that you come across. This one walks in a funny way. That person is not dressed well. You wonder what someone sitting at the park is smiling about. When these thoughts fill your head, you will only drain yourself. Spending too much time focusing on other people will only deter you from using your mind productively. Instead of visualizing your goals and your future, you waste your energy mulling over little things that add no value to you.

## Regular Insomnia

Do you find it hard to sleep sometimes? You may get worked up over the idea that your brain cannot shut down and stop thinking. Sadly, this can paralyze you since your brain doesn't get the rest that it deserves. Gradually, you will notice a decrease in your productivity. You are unlikely to feel good about yourself since there is little that you achieve. Worrying too much about not being able to sleep can make you uneasy and you may find yourself in a state of captivity. If this is something that you have been experiencing, then it sounds like you might be an overthinker. What could you do about this? First, if you are not active, then you must find a way of keeping yourself busy. Also, meditation is a great practice that can help you stop overthinking and relax and focus on the present.

**You Always Live in Fear**

Are you afraid of what the future has in store for you? If you answer yes to this question, then chances are that you're caged in your mind. Living in fear could drive you to resort to drugs and alcohol as your best remedy. You will gain the perception that by taking drugs, it will help you drown your sorrows and help you forget. Unfortunately, this is not the case since drugs and alcohol are mere depressants. They slow down your brain functioning. As a result, you tend to believe that they are helping you forget.

**You're Always Fatigued**

Do you always wake up in the morning feeling tired? This could be a result of stress or depression. Instead of living a productive life, you find yourself waking up late, tired, and unmotivated.

The reason why this happens is because you don't allow your mind to rest. It has been working day and night. In the evening, instead of sleeping you find yourself awake all night because you are overthinking. Your mind cannot work for 24 hours straight at the same level of functioning. You will only suffer from burnouts. You need to give your mind ample time to rest and reboot.

**You Don't Live in the Present**

Do you find it difficult to enjoy life? Why do you think you find it daunting to sit back, relax, and be happy with your friends? The mere fact that you can't stay in the present implies that you won't focus on what is happening in the present. Overthinking will blind you from noticing anything good that is currently happening around you. You will often think about the worst that can happen. The issue is that you are trapped in your mind and there is nothing outside your thoughts that you can constructively think about.

Failure to live in the present denies you the opportunity to improve relationships with other people. You will live in fear that they will criticize you. Therefore, you will only want to exist in your cocoon. Again, this will lead to stress.

**Types of Overthinking**

There are different forms of overthinking that could affect the quality of the decisions we make. Common forms of overthinking are succinctly discussed in the following paragraphs.

## Abstract Thinking

This refers to a form of thinking which goes beyond concrete realities. For instance, when you are trying to formulate theories to explain your observations, then you're engaging in abstract thinking. When your business is not performing well, you might jump to the conclusion that it's because of the economy.

## Complexity

The complexity form of overthinking comes about when there are many factors to consider in your decision-making process. In this case, these numerous factors could prevent you from weighing the true importance of each one of them. The effect is that it could prevent you from making decisions promptly.

## Avoidance

Avoidance occurs when one tries to avoid doing something by using the decision-making process as their excuse.

## Cold Logic

When using cold logic to think, you tend to avoid relying on human factors, including language, culture, personality, emotion, and social dynamics. The outcome is that you end up making biased decisions that do not consider legal or social realities.

## Intuition Neglect

This occurs when one fails to consider what they already know. In other words, one opts to overthink something that they already know a thing or two about. Instead of following your gut instinct, you overthink and end up making the wrong decisions.

## Creating Problems

You may also find yourself thinking in a way where you are creating problems that are not there in the first place. There are certain situations or things that are not as complex as you think. In ordinary situations, it would have taken you a minute or two to solve them. It is vital to focus more on the bigger picture and not nitpick at the details. Sometimes it is important to see things as they are. Don't complicate your life by thinking of potential problems.

## Magnifying the Issue

Usually, small problems require simple solutions. There are instances where we amplify these problems and we end up coming up with overly complex solutions to solve them. This is another form of overthinking. You end up wasting your resources to come up with huge solutions that don't match the problems you are experiencing.

## Fear of Failure

Fear of failure is not a new concept to most people. This is what motivates most of us to work hard. Instead of working hard for a bright future, you find yourself drawing motivation from the fear you have developed inside you.

## Irrelevant Decisions

There are times when we make irrelevant decisions because we force ourselves to make these decisions, yet we are not required to make them. For instance, when thinking about our future, there are instances where we end up making irrelevant decisions based on assumptions. Getting married, for example, based on the assumptions you have, you might conclude that you need to get married because you're getting old.

## Causes of Overthinking

After looking at the possible signs that could indicate you are an overthinker and the types of overthinking, it is important to reflect on the causes. While reading through this section, ask yourself: what causes you to overthink? Frankly, depending on the situation that you might be going through, there are varying reasons why you may think too much. For instance, your fear of embarrassment could push you to overthink what you should wear or how you should present yourself in front of other people. On the other hand, the fear of failure can lead you to work hard towards achieving your goals.

The following are common reasons why you may overthink.

## Lack of Confidence

Lack of confidence is one of the main reasons why people tend to overthink. When you're not sure about what to do, it opens doors for uncertainty. Your mind is filled with fear as a result. It is worth noting that you can never be sure about the decisions that you make. Accordingly, there are times when you will be required to take risks when making important decisions. Taking such risks prevents you from torturing your mind since you will be acting without spending too much time thinking. Deciding to do something gives you confidence. This will have an impact on how you handle problems in your life. With time, you will develop into more of a decision-maker than a thinker.

## Second-Guessing Yourself

Still on the issue of confidence, doubting yourself is mentally exhausting. Sure, it is understandable that you may make the wrong decisions. No one is perfect, so don't expect that you will always make the right choices. However, constantly being indecisive will rob you of your confidence. The main issue here is that you will frequently stress yourself over anything that requires you to make a choice.

To avoid second-guessing yourself, you must trust your abilities. This will be helpful as you will become more self-aware and in turn, end up making sound decisions. The exciting thing is that you will avoid the notion of repeatedly asking other people for their opinions before doing anything.

# Chapter 6 : Correlation of Overthinking with Drinking and Stress Eating

Stress is the state of pressure and tension that a person feels. In this sense, it can be considered a part of daily life. As university students, you may experience stress while trying to meet academic expectations, adapting to the new environment or making new friendships. The stress you experience is not always harmful, even mild stress can be a factor that stimulates you, energizes and improves yourself. However, when your stress level is very high, your productivity may decrease, your pleasure in life may decrease and problems may arise in your relationship with your environment.

Most of us think that stress is caused by external factors such as school, family, friends, disease, but in fact, these factors are not stressful events on their own. What makes them stressful are our comments and internal reactions. People can interpret different events as stressful and react differently to stress. In other words, it is not the external factor that determines stress, but the interaction between him and the person.

**How to Understand the Stress?**

Symptoms that show you that you are experiencing stress can be grouped into four groups: emotional, intellectual, behavioral and physical. You can experience one or more of them at the same time.

**Emotional Symptoms:**

- Feeling anxious or troubled

- Fear or startled quickly

- Feeling worthless, inadequate, insecure or abandoned

- You become irritable or irritable

- Quickly shy

**Intellectual Symptoms:**

- Lack of self-confidence

- Forgetfulness

- Thinking pessimistically

- Your negative fictions about the future

- Your mind is always full of things

- To dream constantly, not to focus your attention

**Behavioral Symptoms:**

- Having difficulty in making decisions that you could easily make before

- Stuttering or other speech difficulties

- Laugh out loud and speak in a nervous tone

- Crying for no reason

- Act without worrying about the consequences

- To   grind your teeth

- Increasing cigarette, drug or alcohol use

- You   tend to crash

**Bodily Symptoms:**

- Your hands or your body, excessive sweating

- Increasing your heart rate

- Your   body shaking

- The   emergence or increase of neural tics

- Having a throat and dry mouth

- Getting tired easily

- You   often go to the toilet

- Having trouble with sleep (too little or too much)

- Having digestive and excretion problems such as diarrhea, indigestion or vomiting

- Having stomach pain or headache

- (Women) Increase of your premenstrual tension

- Your size as well and to be under your back pain

- Losing your appetite or overeating

- Quickly get sick

**Stressful Experiences for Students**

Both positive and negative life events can create stress. Major life changes and some environmental events are important sources of stress that lead many people to seek help. Major life changes that can cause stress include moving, starting a new school or changing school, transitioning to a new job or a new lifestyle, getting married, pregnancy, divorce, separation, death of a relative, dismissal, bankruptcy, chronic diseases. Some environmental events that may cause stress can be listed as time pressure, competition or competition, financial problems, noise and disappointments.

Below are some experiences you may encounter in your university life as a student, you can reduce the stress you may experience if you prepare yourself by knowing them beforehand.

• Adaptation to the Tempo: Difficulties in returning to the disciplined work habits by getting out of the great relaxation when the right to enter the university has been obtained as a result of many years of hard work.

- Adaptation to the new environment: Difficulties in adapting to the new environment, friends and expectations for those who have just started, transitioned to university or return after a certain break. Feeling different but not trying to look different. Do not try to comply with the new environment by continuing to be itself.

- Longing for home: Longing for home, especially for preparatory or freshman students and those who are far from their family. The difficulties of being away from their relatives, especially during important family lives.

- Adopting the learning area: feelings of denial, anger, discontent, indecision and pessimism experienced by students who go to departments that are not particularly sure or do not want much. Researching or trying ways to move to the desired area, these are the frustration, despair and insatiability when they fail. Difficulties in trying to understand and adopt professions that can be entered as a result of education.

- Disappointment: Especially those new students understand that university life is not as perfect as the expectations they have established based on what parents, teachers, friends and the environment tell.

- Loneliness: Feeling depressed about the confusion, vulnerability and lack of support from relatives of trying to adapt to the new environment.

• Social event: An empty or overfilled social calendar. Difficulties in finding, recognizing, participating and actively conducting activities such as in-school student clubs or out-of-school cultural studies that provide attention and develop socially.

• Group of friends: Inability to find a group to belong to or feel sorry to be not chosen or excluded by a group.

• Girlfriend / boyfriend: Students who do not have a girlfriend or boyfriend feel incomplete and inadequate due to the importance of the environment on the flute or loss of self-confidence. Sadness or depression caused by conflict or separation with the girlfriend / boyfriend.

• Deferralism: Continuously postponing and stacking courses with the thought that there is more time. Increased feelings of anxiety and guilt as the deadline for exams and assignments approaches.

• Time balancing: Problems in determining and applying the balanced time and weight to be given to them while fulfilling the requirements of academic, social and private life.

• Success position: Feeling inadequate and unsuccessful due to the difference between the old grades during the high school period and the new grades at the university. Lesson load pressure and distress. Loss of self-esteem that can be caused by the inability to show the perfect success that it expects of itself.

The anxiety of not being able to show the high success expected by the environment.

• Academic pressure: Increasing academic pressure and anxiety of not meeting high expectations. This can push some students to give up completely.

• Perfectionism: Force yourself to be "the best" or to do "the best". Don't expect too much from yourself. Depression and loss of self-confidence when you cannot approach this criterion.

• Substance abuse: Sometimes curiosity, sometimes compliance with the environment, sometimes trying or increasing the use of substances such as cigarettes, alcohol, drugs to feel better or forget about the problem.

• Conflicts of value: Conflict of new experiences with morality, religion and social expectations, and making conscience calculations on value judgments. Switching between different values, the search for identity caused by them.

• Economic hardship: Family benefit, scholarship, and low income earned by the student (for example, working on holidays), difficulty in meeting costs and income balance.

• Holiday pressure: Problems about what to do during a few days of lectures, during the New Year, in the mid-term or during the summer holidays. Anxiety about not being able to use these gaps that are missed well enough. Especially the difficulties experienced by those with familial problems, who do not have homes to visit or who are unable to visit.

• Early work experience: The effort to get work experience during the student in the areas of interest, seeking for it and experiencing inexperience.

• Reading by work: The difficulty of allocating a significant amount of time to business life, balancing and meeting the expectations of academic and business life, due to reasons such as a solution to financial difficulties, lack of interest in the section being studied, and the decision to obtain work experience.

• Job panic / Future anxiety: The rush to find a job for those who are graduating; preparation of professional CV, learning job interview techniques. Anxiety of not finding a job and being idle. Dissatisfaction with the choices that arise, difficulty in making choices between options.

**How Can You Cope with Stress?**

Instead of producing a solution when people are under stress, they often imagine how bad the situation they are in and those they will not change easily. This makes them feel helpless and passive.

Our thoughts and how we interpret an event determine our emotions and behavior. Most of us make some thought mistakes. For example, we make generalizations based on an event, we believe that we know what the other person feels and what they think, we think that our happiness depends on the behavior of other people and we try to change them. However, if we spend our energy to change ourselves, not to change others, we can reach the result in a shorter time.

First of all, you need to review which area (s) of stress arise from your life and what disturbs us in that case, what emotions we experience and how we react with these emotions. Then, thinking about what you can do to change this situation will be an important step in solving the problem.

Many types of stress can be changed, destroyed or reduced. To reduce your stress level, you can:

• It is important to strengthen positive judgments about yourself and focus on your goodness and success, such as "I can deal with this situation", "I will do my best".

• Remember that it is important to experience the present moment. Thinking about the past or the future prevents you from experiencing and enjoying the moment you are in.

• Having to make decisions also creates stress and we delay making decisions. Make a list of what you need to decide and think about what information is needed and how you can get it. Evaluate the pros and cons by considering the options one by one.

• Uncertainties are stressful situations, gather information about them to reduce uncertainties in your life.

• Our values play an important role in the decisions we make, and when we have a conflict in them, stress becomes inevitable. By reviewing your values, you can think about what is important to you in life (success, health, family, friendship, self-esteem, freedom, etc.).

• Most of us are unhappy with the negative since we dream of a smooth life and seek perfect justice in life. "Why did this happen to me?" we think. However, there are some facts that we have to accept. For example, it is unlikely to please everyone or wait for everyone to love and understand us. It is important to have the courage to see and change what we can change while accepting what we cannot change.

• Remember that there is always better and worse. While trying to improve continuously, become aware of your limits and accept them, remember that everyone is unique, one and different. Set realistic goals for yourself. Treat your success in your personal development and avoid unfair and unnecessary competition.

• Develop adverse behavior that protects your rights and that of others. You can say "no".

• Develop a hobby for yourself, relax and have fun, create a time that belongs only to you.

• When  you feel tense, stop, if you can, move away from the tense environment for a while and try to relax by taking a deep breath for a few minutes.

• Maintain a  healthy life and take good care of your body: Do a sport you like regularly, get enough sleep, eat a regular and balanced diet, and stay away from smoking, alcohol and other addictive substances.

•    Share your anxiety and problems with your friends or someone you trust.

•    Achieve engagements to focus on outside of yourself and make a social contribution. Participate in voluntary work on social projects.

•    Use time wisely. To do this, determine your priorities and goals, what work needs to be done first, what works can wait, plan.

•    Study regularly; gradually extend this time starting from short time blocks while working. Take frequent but short breaks.

• When  coping is difficult, seek help from the environment and a specialist, rather than burdening on your borders.

# Chapter 7  : Control Your Thoughts

We all know that technology plays a huge part in people's' lives. We believe it is also a reason for the problem of procrastination. But ironically, it has the answers to your procrastination habits. Since there is technology, you don't have to worry about ending your habit of procrastination. Why? There are numerous ways to overcome the habit of procrastination. Yes, for example, through motivation you can overcome procrastination, but apps and tools sound more practical than motivation. Don't they? So, if you are looking for the best anti-procrastination equipment, know that there are many.

## Small habits, big change

You already know small habits have a bigger impact on your life. For example, if you brush twice a day, you will not see the changes right away, but you will have a great set of teeth when you grow old. Just like that, when you practice simple habits, for now, there will be a massive impact on your life later. So, here are some of the tips that you should follow:

## An organized individual

Do you think plans can't change your level of productivity? Well, try creating a plan, maybe for the work you have for next week or the work you have to complete tomorrow. And then, stick to the plan and see what happens. It might sound simple. You might even wonder if a simple plan can bring so much difference. Well, yes it can! Through a plan, you organize the work that you have to do. When you organize the work, you understand the process clearly. For example, you have to complete a massive project, but if you just let the huge project be as massive as it is, you will not feel like doing it. You will not be able to see the amount of work you have to do in a day and that will create boredom and ignorance. Thus, you have to organize the work that you have. Luckily, there are so many great tools and apps that you can find to organize work (more on this later).

**Make it simple**

Another common reason for procrastination is due to having complex tasks. Of course, some tasks can be complicated, but it is not as if you can't simplify them. For that, you have to set simple, achievable goals. Instead of saying "I'll complete the project" say, "I'll complete the first part of the project today." When you make it sound simple, it will be simple.

**Have a schedule**

Once you have a goal, it is important to schedule it because scheduled work has a higher rate of achievement. Break your work into chunks and set a deadline. If you set your deadline, you will be able to achieve them before the actual deadline boggles your mind. Sometimes, you might come across unexpected situations in life, thus, completing the work before the deadline will help you stay in the safe zone.

## Set aside distractions

You might already know the things that distract you. For example, if you are addicted to Snapchat, don't keep it your phone near you until you get the work done. Or if you are a LinkedIn enthusiast like me, stay offline until you complete the work. Don't even add the Google chrome extension of LinkedIn because it is incredibly distracting. The moment you see the notification, you might want to check the messages even if you have so much to do. Thus, it is better to put all your distractions aside and focus on the work you have.

## The Pomodoro Technique

If you don't know what this means, this approach promotes working for 25 minutes and taking a break for 5 minutes. Most people consider this as an effective and excellent solution for procrastination. Honestly, this is a fantastic technique, and you will be able to get a lot of things done if you follow this approach. Moreover, by following this technique, you can ensure the quality of your work as well. During the break, you must not get distracted, thus do something like listening to music, walking, or even screaming to release stress. Whatever it may be, make sure it makes you feel relaxed and comfortable. Thus, the activity that you chose to do should be something that you like, but not will divert your focus!

## Reward yourself

I don't think anybody hates rewards, so it is highly recommended to reward yourself when you follow your plan. For example, if you set a goal to write 2500 words within 5 hours, you must treat yourself once you have achieved it! You can reward yourself with ice cream or an episode of your favorite show. However, make sure that you'll get back to your routine once you've rewarded yourself.

## The myth of doing the hard thing

So far, you have probably heard that doing the hard things first, help you get other things done sooner. REALLY? Let me ask that again, REALLY? The rule of doing the hard things first don't work for me. If it works for you, then, please ignore this point. But if you really give it a thought, you will understand the underlying concept. When you do what's possible, you become motivated to do the hard things too. Besides, when you try to the hard tasks and if it looks harder than it seemed, you might even delay the work. Thus, it is usually better to do things that are manageable first.

These are the small habits and changes that you must incorporate to become a productive individual. But there are many more anti-procrastination tips that I want to share with you.

**Getting started technique**

If you want to do something, you must get started. People usually procrastinate at the beginning of a project, so it is important to understand the techniques to get started. How can you do it? Starting a project or a task will not be easy; in fact, it can be the reason for delayed submission. Whenever you plan to do a task, you need something to boost your mood. At first, getting started can be difficult, but when you move on with the task, it might seem possible. Thus, compare the way you feel when you start the work and the way you feel when you delay the work.

Even if you have done a little from the whole project, it's a good start. Starting the project is important, so it doesn't matter even if you do a very little portion of the whole project. There is a trick to make your mind like the work, and that is to start thinking about the work. When you keep your mind occupied with the task, you might somehow end up starting it. The reason is it is tiring to think, so you eventually start work.

For example, say you should edit an article. If you don't begin editing, you will never do it. Thus, just take the draft and change a few words. Eventually, you'll end up changing the major sections where you wanted to change. You will do it even without forcing yourself to do it, which is amazing!

Or you can set a timer. What can you do with a timer if you really can't start the work? Simple, set the timer to 10 minutes or less and then, once the timer starts working you just remain seated. Even if you don't do the work, just sit there. Eventually, you'll start work, and you will not even feel that you have started. This is an easy trick because when you are within your workspace, you can't help, but work.

Thus, these tricks and tips might help you get better at what you are doing. The simplest mantra is "get started!"

## Useful Tools and Apps

Now that you've learned almost all the possible trips and tricks, it is time to get a grip on the tools and apps available. Beating procrastination will not be easy until you get help from the technology that you blamed for your reluctance. You have so many great tools and apps to select from, yet we'll discuss a few beneficial tools that you can rely on. Here we go!

## Procraster

This is one of the procrastination-busting apps, but compatible only for iPad and iPhone. The app will support you throughout the procedures by providing the right answers and advice as to the option that you provide. For example, if you select the option

"I don't know how to start" the app will suggest breaking the tasks into chunks. It provides not only ideas but also guidance to do the work. You'll find a rhythm to your work, and you can even check the statistics related to your productivity. The statistics will become a motivation to reach the goals.

## StandStand

Anecdotally, it is considered that changes in the working environment can cause positive changes to your productivity. Thus, the introduction of the portable standing working table has become a great piece of equipment to fight against procrastination. Sometimes, you might get bored by sitting for long hours, in such a case, you can consider the StandStand table. The StandStand table helps to increase productivity by allowing you to alternate between sitting and standing at your workstation. Once you change your posture, you'd be able to do focus and get a lot of things done. This is available for purchase on Amazon.

## Focuswriter

If you want to type something on the laptop or computer screen, you must make sure that you don't get distracted. It is easy to get distracted when you have the option to open as many as tabs as you want. While working on screen, if you have too many tabs open it will definitely kill your productivity. So, for that Focuswriter is a great tool. This is a program that works exactly like a Word document. It also has built-in timers, better ambiance, daily goals, and many other options. This program supports Windows, Mac, and Linux systems. By using this tool, you will be able to do your work on time with better productivity. Moreover, the time that you usually kill can be saved.

**Freedom**

This app provides peace of mind by helping you focus on the important things and avoiding distractions. Once the app does it for you, you will be able to focus on the work you do. People often procrastinate when they slowly shift from an important task to another entertaining activity. For example, say that you are working on a project, but meanwhile, you are scrolling through Facebook feeds, so do you really think that you can give your best to work? I don't think so. When your attention is divided among other unimportant tasks, you will not be able to give the best to your MOST important project. So, the Freedom app will help you by blocking sites such as Twitter, Facebook, and so on. The Freedom app will block almost all the time-consuming sites. So, there's no reason why you must not consider it.

**Todoist**

This is one of the popular apps that you might have often come across. People usually procrastinate because of not having a proper plan. Or not knowing the task to do next. If you have a structured plan, you will be able to understand the task that you must do next. So, with the help of the Todoist app, you can get the structure of the plan. You can use this app to track and sync the tasks to your mobile and other devices. The app is available for Android, Windows Phone, iOS, and the web. Once you download the app to your device, you will be able to get the To-Do-List!

**Write or Die**

This is an excellent app for the ones who can't overcome procrastination even after changing their behavior. If you are still struggling to focus even after changing your behaviors, you must take extreme measurements. The app Write or Die will avoid procrastination by sending annoying pictures and sounds. This is called Kamikaze mode (derived from the term created from Japanese suicide pilots during World War II). When you delay work, the vowels on your documents will automatically be deleted. Perhaps, you wouldn't prefer deleting the words you hardly type. Thus, this can be one of the best anti-procrastination equipment.

**Spotify**

This app will help you stay entertained while you are working. Whenever you find it boring to get your work done, you can play some great music on Spotify. This might help you avoid procrastination. Besides, if you play some motivational songs, you'll be driven to do the work.

**Tomato Timer**

I mentioned about Pomodoro Technique earlier, and this app relates to it. You usually procrastinate when you don't feel like doing a big task. But you still have to get this task done, and for that, you have to divide the big task into smaller tasks. The Tomato Timer app is the idea to help you to get things done by dividing them into chunks. You just have to set a timer, and then, you will be able to get the work done.

Even though there are many more tools and apps that you can consider, these are treated as the most important and beneficial ones! Select the most suitable tool or app as per your preferences and make use of it!

# Chapter 8 : Declutter Your Life

We live in a world that requires us to act on many things. Besides overcoming daily stressors, we should learn how to develop the right habits that prevent us from worrying and thinking negative thoughts. The strenuous environment and the hustle and bustle we have to face often fills our minds with clutter. It often reaches a point where our minds can't stop thinking. You may become overwhelmed with thoughts that leave your mind in a total mess. Does this sound like you? If yes, then your mind is waving a white flag at you and may require some decluttering.

In the same way that you will regularly spare some time to declutter your office and your house, the mind also requires decluttering. This will guarantee that you free up some space for optimal functioning. However, it is not as easy as it sounds since you cannot see exactly what is in the mind. As a result, the cleaning process will be different from the normal decluttering that you have been used to. So, how do you empty the unnecessary from your mind? This chapter will focus on answering this question and it will help you understand the significance of decluttering your mind.

## Causes of Mental Clutter

In an ordinary case, when cleaning your home or office, you will start by identifying the items that are causing clutter. Likewise, before decluttering your mind, you must start by identifying the causes of mental clutter. The importance of doing this is that it guarantees that you can effectively deal with clutter in the long run. You will be more aware of the factors that contribute to clutter in your mind and work to avoid them.

The following are some of the common causes of mental clutter.

## Overwhelm

Naturally, if you are overwhelmed with things, then it will lead to disorder in your mind. As a result, it will be daunting for you to establish a reasonable way of dealing with your issues. This causes clutter. Fortunately, you can overcome this by acknowledging the fact that you can't handle everything at once. This means that you should break down your tasks into smaller, yet manageable mini-tasks. Handle these things one at a time. At the end of the day, you will realize that there is a lot that you have accomplished without feeling overwhelmed.

## Over-Commitment

Committing yourself to finish certain activities on your to-do list is a good thing. Nonetheless, when you can't say no to other assignments, it means that you are over-committing yourself. Handling too many things will only lead to frustration. This is because there is a probability that you might fail to deliver.

Learning to say no is an essential attribute of living a productive life. Saying no shouldn't be considered a bad thing since you're committing yourself to work productively on what you can manage. So, avoid over-committing yourself and taking on more than you can handle.

**Fear**

If you're afraid to let go of what has happened in the past, then are likely to strain your mind. The habit of holding on to things and thoughts often consumes us. Instead of working productively, your mind will keep ruminating on the past. This is pure clutter. Why should you put yourself through this torture when you can simply learn to let go?

**Emotional Overload**

Maybe your mind is filled with unwanted thoughts and feelings that keep draining energy from you. For instance, you might be dealing with a looming family crisis and it ends up affecting your productivity at work. If this is what you are going through, then you should find time to deal with the issue. Ask for a leave of absence and free your mind from having to think over this matter repeatedly.

**Lack of Time**

Time will always be a prevalent issue. In everything that you do, you will often feel as though you don't have enough time. The reality is that there is enough time to handle all the important things in your life if you prioritize and plan effectively. Therefore, you shouldn't use the excuse that you lack time. The only issue here is that you may not know how to effectively manage your time. Organize yourself and prioritize what needs to be done first. This way, you will have more time to handle pending tasks on your to-do list.

## Procrastination

If you are a victim of procrastination, then it comes as no surprise that your mind is always in a state of overdrive. Pushing things to be done at a later time means that there is a lot that will require your attention when 'later' comes. After a while, you will feel overwhelmed that you cannot complete everything on time. The problem began with the decision to procrastinate.

## A Major Change in Life

Another reason why your mind might be filled with clutter is because of a major change that has occurred in your life. Frankly, sometimes we have to acknowledge the fact that change is inevitable. People fail to embrace change in their lives. As a result, they spend too much time doing what they used to do instead of changing. When faced with such predicaments, you must evaluate what's going on in your life and strive to change.

Familiarity with the causes of mental clutter is the first step towards successful mental decluttering. Once you are aware of what causes clutter in your mind, you can develop practical solutions of how to get rid of them. It is worth bearing in mind that in most cases, there are multiple reasons why your mind is cluttered. So, open up your mind when trying to identify the factors that cause your messy mental state.

## Practical Tips on How to Declutter Your Mind

Now that you understand what's causing all the clutter, let's look at some of how you can declutter your mind.

## Set Priorities

Sometimes we fail to realize that a life without goals is a boring life. Living a goalless life is like wandering in the forest forever without a map. You don't have a particular destination that you want to reach. What's worse, you don't even know how to maneuver through the forest. Similarly, life without goals has no meaning. Your daily activities will be consumed with people and activities that don't add value to you. You will live in your comfort zone since there is nothing that you're targeting to achieve.

Setting priorities is a good place to start when looking to declutter your mind. This requires that you sit down and identify things that matter the most to your life. List down these goals and work to ensure that your actions are in line with the set goals. Setting priorities create structure with your to-do lists. You will begin to value the importance of delegating tasks when you feel like you can't handle them. More importantly, you will learn to say no since you comprehend the significance of handling only what you value and what you can take on.

## Keep a Journal

Keeping a journal is a great strategy to help organize your thoughts. People tend to underestimate the power of noting down their thoughts every day. Journaling helps you rid your mind from things that you might not be aware of. It enhances your working memory and also guarantees that you can effectively manage stress. Similarly, the habit of noting down your daily experiences in a journal helps you express your emotions that may be bottled up within you. Therefore, you create space to experience new things in life. The effect of this is that you can relieve yourself from the anxiety that you might have been experiencing.

## Learn to Let Go

Decluttering your mind can also be made easier if you learn to let go. Holding on to things in the past adds little or no value to your life. It only affects your emotional and mental wellbeing. The mere fact that you cannot let go implies that you will find it daunting to look ahead. Your mind will stagnate and this will stress you out. If you were a bird and you wanted to fly, what would you do? Without a doubt, you would want to free yourself from any burden that weighs you down. Apply this to real life and free yourself from any emotional baggage that you might be holding on to. Whether it's your failed past relationships or failed job opportunities, just let go. There is a greater reward in letting go since you open doors for new opportunities in your life.

## Breathe

Breathing exercises would also help clear clutter from your mind. Certain forms of meditation depend on breathing exercises to focus your attention on the breath. So, how do you practice breathing exercises? Start by taking a slow deep breath. Pause for a moment before exhaling. While breathing in and out, focus your mind on how you are breathing. Concentrate on how your breath goes in and out of your nose. It's relaxing, right? Practicing breathing exercises more often relaxes your mind. Besides helping you to relax, it boosts your immune system in profound ways.

## Declutter Your Physical Environment

If you live in a messy house, then there is a good chance that you're more likely frustrated. This may be because you find it difficult to find things you need. For instance, you end up wasting a lot of time looking for your car keys before heading to work. This affects how you start your day. You will be stressed that you arrived late and that numerous tasks are waiting for you. Therefore, decluttering your physical space will also have a positive impact on your mind. Keeping things organized also means that your mind is virtually organized to handle the things that ought to be handled.

## Learn to Share Your Thoughts

There is an overall positive feeling when you sit down to share your feelings with someone you care about. Instead of holding back your tears and emotions, sharing your feelings with your loved ones can clear emotional clutter from your mind. Have you ever wondered why you can think more clearly after sharing your sad feelings with another person? There is power in sharing your thoughts and feelings with other people. You can be more certain that you are making informed decisions since your mind can think clearly without being blinded by your emotions.

## Curb Your Information Intake

The information that we consume affects the quality of the decisions we make. Unfortunately, the information we consume is sometimes unimportant to our lives. It only fills our minds with clutter and this prevents us from thinking clearly and making the right decisions. The worst thing is that it causes anxiety and stress as we tend to worry about the worst that could happen to us after what we have read or watched over the internet. Limiting what you consume from the internet can help prevent unwanted information from taking up space in your mind. So, instead of starting your day by checking your social media page, consider going for a walk or reading a book. The point here is that you should substitute your unproductive time on the internet by doing productive things.

## Spare Some Time to Unwind

More importantly, to declutter your mind, you should consider taking a break. You might believe that taking breaks is unproductive, but the truth is that your productivity can be given a huge boost when you take breaks more often. Giving yourself some time to unwind helps you recharge. As a result, you end up doing more in less time. This is what effectiveness and efficiency are all about. They both account for your productivity.

## The Importance of Decluttering Your Mind

Decluttering the physical space around you will help you create more space for more important things. Such tidiness will also have an impact on your mind since everything will be organized and you will know where everything is. Few things are reminding you that they need to be arranged. Likewise, decluttering your mind also has its benefits.

## A Decrease in Stress and Anxiety

Clutter will stress you out. Feeling like your mind is messy may make you feel tired since there is a lot to do yet so little time. Similarly, mental clutter will also make you feel unconfident.

You will rarely be confident about your abilities. Repeatedly, you will notice that you second-guess everything that you do. All this is happening because your mind can't think straight. There is a lot that it is focusing on and therefore, finding practical solutions to the little things ahead of you may seem impossible.

By using the recommended strategies discussed herein to clear the clutter from your mind, you can be more equipped to lower your stress and anxiety levels. Your mind will feel more liberated. The new space that you have created will give your mind the energy it needs to think and make smart decisions. As a result, you will feel more confident about yourself and the decisions that you make.

**An Improvement in Your Productivity**

Clutter can prevent your mind from achieving the focus it needs to handle the priorities that you have set for yourself. For instance, instead of waking up early and working on an important project, you might find yourself paying too much attention to the emotional burden that is weighing you down. Frankly, this thwarts your level of productivity. You are unlikely to use your time wisely, which affects your productivity.

Eliminating unwanted thoughts and emotions will help you focus more on what is important. You will find it easier to set priorities and work towards them. You will wake up feeling motivated and goal-oriented. In the short run, you will notice an improvement in your efficiency. Over time, you will realize that you're more effective than ever before since there is more that you can do in less time.

**Enhanced Emotional Intelligence**

There are numerous situations in which we allow our emotions to affect how we perceive things in life. One minute you love someone and the next minute you think that they are the worst and you regret ever meeting them. Also, these emotions cloud our judgment and we end up making conclusions that are not valid. In most cases, this occurs when there is a lot on our minds that we have to handle. The result is that we fail to deal with these emotions effectively.

Decluttering your mind requires that you get rid of negative thoughts that would lead to negative emotions. As a result, decluttering more often implies that you will master how to deal with negative feelings. You are less likely to allow negative feelings to weigh you down. This is because you understand that they are just emotions and letting them go is the best course of action you can take.

You can transform your life by choosing to declutter your mind. You will end up making better decisions that lead your life in the right direction. However, it is important to note that the decluttering process will only be successful if you know where the clutter is coming from. To start, you can evaluate yourself and find out why there is so much clutter in your mind. Is it because you overcommit yourself? Is it because you are overwhelmed with the challenges that you have to handle? Is it caused by your fear of making mistakes? Knowing the reasons for clutter ensures that you can control clutter in the long haul. Also, the digital age that we're living in should not be an excuse to fill your mind with unwanted information. Feed your mind with quality information that drives you to achieve your goals. Curb your information intake and free yourself from clutter.

# Chapter 9 : Practicing Mindfulness

Mindfulness is a practice of being present, not just for a minute or two, but throughout the day, every day, for your life. The goal is to maintain mindfulness all the time, though we all accept that we are not computers or robots and there will be times when we lose focus or our minds fill up with other emotions and feelings that take us away in reaction to life events. A parallel can be drawn with a religious mindset. In the Christian mindset, followers accept that they are human and will make mistakes, while at the same time doing their best each day to maintain a sinless, righteous, and faithful existence. Just because we know we will make mistakes; doesn't mean we don't try. And this is why the long-term effects emotionally, spiritually, physically, and emotionally are well worth our efforts. So, let's look at what mindfulness has to offer us and then we'll learn how you can integrate the practice into your own life.

Think about how you feel after you successfully banish a needless or hurtful thought and replace it with a new, positive one. It makes you feel good, right? And it also gives you a sense of clarity, like a big mess has just been cleaned up from the floor of your mind. The same thing happens when we learn to practice mindfulness. Only with mindfulness, there is a bonus.

Practicing mindfulness consistently leads to a feeling of potential, of hope, and of looking forward with a fresh pair of eyes. You are moving forward with a clear mind and you are taking stock of each second that passes you by. So, when I talk about a feeling of potential and looking forward, I'm not talking about looking forward to the next day or weekend or month. I'm talking about moving forward, step by step, minute by minute, feeling and seeing everything around you and feeling each moment as it passes. There is a feeling of happiness and satisfaction that follows because you are getting rid of the thoughts that have no use for you at this moment. And your mind is thanking you.

Your heart and soul are thanking you. There is so much to sense and be grateful for here and now. Mindfulness is all about bringing in your perspective to these close quarters, small-scale way of thinking, and in the process, the whole world opens up to you.

So, how do you start practicing mindfulness? Well, the biggest task here is going to be honing the skill of focus. But there's good news. If you've been able to practice the interruption technique and replace your negative thoughts and emotions with positive ones, then you've already done a lot to cultivate this skill. Focus comes from the mental effort of sharpening your thinking and scaling it down to a single task without letting your mind wander all over the place to things that are not helping you perform that task. As I've discussed before, you don't want to fall into the trap of trying so hard that this exercise becomes a chore and a source of worry for you. Everyone new and first being introduced to mindfulness is going to move forward and improve at a different pace because we are unique human beings. And that's perfectly ok. As with everything else in this book, the key is to take small steps at a time.

A good exercise in practicing mindfulness is simply to go outside and experience nature. Go to an area of a park that is generally quiet and take a seat at a bench or a picnic table. Take a few deep breaths and quiet your mind. Give yourself a minute or two to accomplish this. While you begin focusing your mind, listen to the sounds going on around you, the dogs barking, or the wind blowing through the trees. Feel the breeze on your face or the heat from the sun beating down on you. Feel your body in space. Make sure you are sitting in a comfortable position. Close your eyes as you begin. Then, as you start to appreciate and focus only on what's around you, slowly open your eyes. Look around and take in what you see without forming thoughts around them. Again, this may not come naturally, but gradually with practice. Appreciate the beauty around you, whatever it is you see. If you don't have a nice park to go to, you can do the same exercise in your backyard or neighborhood. Listen to the birds or the kids playing down the street. Try to focus only on sensations without forming thoughts about them or letting your mind wander. As you make time to practice mindfulness just for a few minutes each day, you will start to notice that it is getting easier the more you practice.

## Meditation

A discussion on mindfulness follows naturally into a discussion of meditation because they are closely related. To me, they are part of each other while indicating different practices.

Meditation, for many people, translates to practicing mindfulness throughout every day. To others, meditation means a dedicated space of time each day or week that is used for formal meditation practice from a specific school of thought or philosophy. For example, Zen Buddhism. I will mention a few different styles of meditation but will be discussing Zen in particular because it is the form with which I am most familiar.

The same exercises you've practiced in nature can be applied to a practice of meditation. Since most people associate meditation with the image of sitting in a quiet room with your eyes closed, let's look at how you can start practicing meditation in your own home by following a few simple steps.

Depending on your physical ability, find a comfortable position where you can sit with your back relatively straight. Your arms should be relaxed at your sides, and your neck should not be strained. A simple Google search will go through the more formal sitting structure if you are interested in this, but for right now, we will take a casual approach to the physical technique and focus more on what's going on inside your mind.

When we discussed mindfulness, we talked about sensing the world around you and concentrating only on what is happening to you in the moment. Meditation is similar, except that, in the discipline of Zen meditation, the goal is not to restrict one's thoughts, but instead to resist sticking to individual thoughts as they enter and exit your mind. The core emphasis is still to focus on the present, but the philosophy of Zen is to not restrict the mind but to instead free the mind and let it remain fluid while returning consistently to the present experience.

To illustrate this, have you ever caught yourself or a friend has caught you zoning out, staring blankly in front of you, while your mind drifts and starts to have a dialogue with itself regarding something you said yesterday or something embarrassing you might have done years ago? The thought process has taken you completely out of the present, and now you are lost in a replay of moments that have already happened, things that cannot be changed. But still, you dwell on those moments as mistakes and worry about what people think about you, while in reality, they probably don't even remember those insignificant events. Sound familiar? We all do it. The ultimate goal in meditation is to avoid those sticky thoughts that try their best to take us out of the present and into the past or the future—spaces that either cannot be changed or that we cannot predict. The brain likes to know things and form patterns to predict and make sense of our lives. But we can get wrapped up in this to the point that we miss life as it is happening in the present.

Zen is all about acknowledging the wandering nature of the mind but also accepting the core principle of impermanence—everything changes, even the thoughts in your mind. Dwelling on a single thought or feeling or emotion is useless and irrelevant in an impermanent world and will only hold you at a standstill.

This may not make perfect sense yet, and if you need to start with the absolute basics, go back to that phrase we brought up at the beginning of this chapter—

Just "pay attention." Look around, feel yourself in space, listen, appreciate. That's all you need to focus on to get started. As with all of these positive habits, you will soon form a new addiction to the positivity that mindfulness offers. After this point, meditation will follow naturally.

As I mentioned, meditation can take many forms and you should not feel like there is one right way to meditate. Many practice mindfulness and meditation through movement to music called dance meditation. Other people, including Zen Buddhist monks, practice "walking meditation." Movement often helps regulate and soothe the mind as we introduce patterns of movement that flow just like the free-flowing of our thoughts. Whatever your style and preference, just remember why you're practicing in the first place, and there is no "doing it wrong."

## Positive Thinking

Positive thinking links right in with the thought technique where we were interrupting negative thoughts and introducing positive ones. But with positive thinking, the idea is to cultivate the positive thoughts first, instead of waiting and using them as a reaction to negative thoughts. This is another practice that will look different from person to person. It also should not be an overwhelming concept that discourages you from trying it.

Simply put, positive thinking means you practice waking up and thinking about each day as a fresh, new, unpredictable day rather than dreading what you think you know is already going to happen. Nobody knows the future, and even if your routine seems pretty set in stone when you form the habit of dreading something each day in connection to work (which is something I hope you've already addressed!), then you close yourself off to experiencing surprising things or things that would give you joy. You may recognize what I'm talking about with an example. Think of Mr. Scrooge from the classic Christmas tale, "A Christmas Carol." It's Christmas eve and there are children laughing and playing in the snow, people shopping and sharing Christmas cards and talking joyfully with strangers. But then there is Mr. Scrooge trudging through the snow toward his office, already determining that Christmas is a terrible time and there is no happiness to be found in it—only loss of money. Because he's already determined that he will not be enjoying Christmas, he is unable to open his heart to the joy going on all around him.

Similarly, when we wake up and dread what is going to happen that day, we become blind to the events that would offer joy and surprise and happiness. Did you know that people receive subtle signals not to engage or talk to you when you are upset or unhappy? Think of all the fun spontaneous conversations you've had at work when you arrive in a good mood, positive, and open to whatever the day will throw at you. Let this thought be a motivation for you to try cultivating positive thinking every day, at the beginning of the day.

## Cultural Backing for the Effects of Positive Thinking

You may or may not remember the phenomenon of the "law of attraction" as it was popularized through releases like The Secret. Many believe that positive thinking works to attract positive events and effects in your life when you practice consistently. You've probably heard the saying, "if you put your mind to it, you can accomplish anything." This is what positive thinking and the law of attraction is all about.

It may help to journal about your experience as you practice this skill. Think of a goal for your life. Maybe it's a goal you've had for years and years, or maybe it's something you just thought about today. Write down your goal in your journal and write a little bit about what accomplishing that goal might look like for you. Perhaps you see yourself with a family and friends at a big party as you celebrate a promotion, or you've set aside time for a family vacation to the Bahamas. Maybe you're visualizing yourself having lost 30 pounds in that new bathing suit you've had your eye on for a long time. Whatever your goal, the idea here is to write out the experience with as much detail as you can imagine. Make it real in your mind, then write down what you see.

Next, you'll want to write down the steps on the pathway toward your goal. Positive thinking is a powerful tool, but to make your goal a reality, you're also going to need to put in the work. What do you need to do between now and next year that will help you reach your promotion? What plan do you have in place to follow to lose weight safely and in a way that you can sustain?

If you watch movie awards shows, you may be familiar with the speech many of the winners give in which they attest to visualizing and thinking about their dreams for years before they achieved what they wanted to achieve.

If you let yourself get depressed and convince yourself you can never accomplish something, then you definitely will not accomplish it. Practicing positive thinking will naturally carry you closer and closer to your goals, because you are motivating yourself, consciously and subconsciously, to be ready for those opportunities that you would probably miss with a negative mindset. Just like Scrooge and his blindness to joy, it is possible to wrap yourself so tightly in the negativity that you don't see an opportunity right in front of you.

Practice positive thinking and mindfulness in small steps every day, and soon it will become easy and natural to continue. The joy and freedom that comes with practice like this is something your mind and body and spirit will begin to crave. Just like when you exercise and your body thanks you with all those positive feelings from endorphins and a sense of accomplishment, your mind and body will thank you with positive feelings for the future and it will become hard to resist the pull of positivity.

Don't take my word for it. If you work hard to cultivate and maintain these positive changes in your life, I'm positive you'll hear about it from those closest to you as they witness the changes happening. It may even motivate them to learn more about mindfulness, meditation, and positive thinking to make these practices an important part of their lives as well.

# Chapter 10: How to Solve Overthinking and The Correlated Problems

A cluttered mind has no space for anything new. Often, when you feel that your mind is in a state of overdrive, it prevents you from enjoying the opportunities that life has to offer. Overthinking will put you in a constant loop since you feel like you can't stop yourself from ruminating over a certain issue. The worst thing about this is that there is minimal action you can take to solve the challenge that you are experiencing. As a result, overthinking only damages you as it holds you back from living your life to the fullest. This chapter looks at practical tips that you can incorporate into your life to help you stop overthinking.

## Learn to be Aware

Just like any other problem that you might be going through, the best way of solving it is by understanding the causes of the problem in the first place. Concerning overthinking, the first step towards dealing with it is by recognizing that you are overthinking. You must live consciously by knowing what is happening in your mind. Any time you feel overwhelmed and stressed, you should take a moment to analyze the situation that you are going through. Your awareness should denote to you that these thoughts roaming in your mind are not helpful.

Enhancing your level of self-awareness will help you stop yourself from thinking too much.

The following pointers should help you to boost your self-awareness.

**Meditate**

Today, millions of people value the importance of meditation. Usually, meditation stresses the aspect of focusing on a certain mantra or your breathing. Meditating regularly increases your self-awareness since you connect with your inner-self in ways that you haven't done before. Meditation will help you connect with your inner self. Accordingly, practicing self-talk keeps you motivated on the goals that you have set for yourself.

**Know Your Strengths and Weaknesses**

Another effective way of increasing your self-awareness is by knowing your strengths and coping with your weaknesses. Undeniably, as humans, we are not perfect. The strengths and weaknesses that we have, affect how we work towards our goals. In this regard, most people will only focus on doing the things that they are good at while doing their best to ignore their weaknesses. Knowing yourself better ensures that you don't waste your time and energy doing activities that will only make you feel negatively about yourself.

**Know Your Emotional Triggers**

Also, you must know the emotional triggers that frequently influence your reactions. By knowing these triggers, you can catch yourself before overreacting. Moreover, your self-awareness can be helpful here as it guarantees that your emotions do not overwhelm you. Instead of reacting without thinking twice, you can stop to mull over a particular scenario and act accordingly.

**Practice Self-Discipline**

Every day, your life will revolve around things that you wish to accomplish. Achieving set goals can be a very positive experience. However, this doesn't come easily. You have to be willing to pay the price. This means that you should learn how to effectively control yourself and focus on what's more important. This is what self-discipline is all about. You should be ready to do anything that brings you closer to your goals.

**Try New Experiences**

There is a lot that you can gain from life when you learn to value the importance of new experiences. Think about it this way - the more you know, the more you find different ways of approaching life and solving the problems you are facing. Don't limit yourself by going through life with the same perceptions and doing the same things over and over again. Frankly, this will make every aspect of your life boring. So, go out and have fun. Try new things and challenges.

## Motivate Yourself

We all need motivation at some point in life. When you are motivated to do something, your mind has the energy it needs to see through a particular challenge. Therefore, motivation warrants that you embrace positivity despite the problems that you might be going through. Indeed, this also has an impact on your self-awareness since you are surer about yourself and your abilities.

## Get a Second Opinion

Earlier on, we had pointed out the fact that overthinking can be caused by overcommitting yourself. Maybe this is something that you are accustomed to. We all know how it feels when you manage to complete a project on your own. However, at times it is important to recognize that you can't do everything alone. As you might have heard, "two heads are better than one." Save yourself from the nightmare of weighing your options on something over and over again. Just ask someone else for a second opinion. You will be surprised that you can easily solve a problem that once appeared too difficult for you. Therapy works in the same manner since you get an opportunity to talk over your thoughts with an expert.

## Stay Positive

When you are constantly worried that something could go wrong, your mind will race through varying thoughts trying to figure out the best possible solution to solve your situation. Instead of paying too much attention to the negative, change your thoughts and reflect on all the good things that can happen to you. Savor these moments and help your mind adjust to the fact that you can also be happy. Develop a habit of encouraging your thoughts to stay positive.

## Identify Distractions

There is a common phrase that goes "what you resist persists." In line with the habit of overthinking, trying to prevent yourself from thinking about something only makes you think too much about it. As a result, the best way of stopping this is by doing something more engaging. Go for a walk with friends. Learn to play a new musical instrument. The point here is that you should make an effort to distract your mind.

## Stop Being a Perfectionist

There is a good feeling that comes with knowing that you have done something perfectly. Nevertheless, it is quite demanding to do things perfectly all the time. In your everyday life, you should leave room for mistakes. This ascertains that you will not be frustrated when something goes wrong. Focus on learning from your mistakes. Ultimately, you will notice that you start paying less attention to doing things perfectly. This creates room for more opportunities since you will be willing to try anything, whether you succeed or not.

## Set Deadlines

Spending too much time thinking about a decision can lead to overthinking. Some decisions do not require you to think too much about them. They are simple choices that you can make within a short period. Therefore, it makes sense to set deadlines that you will make a specific decision before the end of the day. Depending on the importance of the decision, you should set ample time to ensure you end up making sound decisions.

## Surround Yourself with the Right People

At times, it is difficult to think positively if the people you surround yourself with frequently have negative thoughts. If you spend most of your time with people who are always worrying, then you can be sure that you will also find yourself worrying. On the contrary, if you surround yourself with people who always think positively, you will also be influenced to have this perception about your dreams and aspirations. Therefore, you can help stop overthinking by choosing to spend time with productive and positive people. They will help free your mind from worrying about what the future holds for you. With their positive energy, you will appreciate the importance of living in the present.

## Do Your Best

When facing new challenges in life, it is a common thing to see most people worry about what they can and cannot do.

Unfortunately, this worrying attitude prevents people from handling challenging situations effectively. When faced with difficult situations, it is imperative to focus on giving it your best without thinking too much as to whether you got it right or not. You never know, there are certain situations when the outcome is not as important as you thought.

**Create a To-Do List**

We can attest to the fact that there are instances when the mind tends to blow things out of proportion. Have you ever heard your inner voice try and convince you that you cannot complete a certain project within a specified period of time? Frankly, this happens many times where the mind jumps to the conclusion that you have more things to do than you do. The funny thing is that the mind will even go to the extent of giving you reasons why you cannot complete the project. To prevent this from happening, you should learn how to work using a to-do list. A to-do list keeps things organized. It guarantees that you can handle one task at a time without making it seem too burdensome for your mind to tackle.

**Cut Yourself Some Slack**

The desire to succeed might be too ingrained in you that you cannot think of anything else that is not related to what you want. This leads to a scenario where you are too hard on yourself. You will find it difficult to forgive yourself for the little mistakes that you make along the way. Unfortunately, this leads to overthinking.

The truth is that you can't always expect that things will go your way. We are human beings and therefore, we are prone to making mistakes. Successful people understand the importance of making mistakes. It allows them to identify their weaknesses and work on them before reaching their goals. Imagine if people only succeeded without making mistakes. Mistakes should be perceived as a stepping stone towards success. As such, always remember that being too hard on yourself is damaging.

On a final note on how to stop overthinking, you should bear in mind that anyone can be a victim of overthinking. We all yearn for the best in life. Therefore, it is okay to overthink things from time to time. However, this becomes a problem when it develops into a habit and you feel as though you cannot do anything about it. The practical tips discussed in this section should help you catch yourself when you think too much. Your self-awareness, for example, will come handy each time you slip into a state of overthinking. Additionally, looking for positive distractions can encourage your mind to think about other things instead of sinking into your thoughts. More importantly, you should always remember to seek a second opinion from those around you. There is a good reason why we have friends and social circles. They should be there to help you offload thoughts and emotions that seem to weigh you down. Talk to your loved ones and if there is no one to talk to, you can always engage in self-talk.

# Chapter 11 : How to Be Positive

The life you live today is contributed by the habits you have. Habits results to all the success you have achieved. For example, your health, moods, and achievements have been successful because of habits. The activities you take part in shape your life. If, for instance, you engage in bad habits continuously, the bad habits will destroy your life. If you decide to implement good habits, this can change your life forever. It depends on one if he chooses to change his life, then he will make the changes unbeneficial behaviors and replace them with what will benefit him in terms of behaviors. Don't despise the small changes that may take part because they make a great difference in the life of somebody.

Establishing good habits and behaviors takes time to implement; it is not something that will happen in seconds. There methods that can help you to implement the desired behaviors. The following method can be used to help one build new habits:

**Setting a Trigger**

This is having intentions to change the habits and increasing the likelihood of forming a new habit and implementing it. For instance, if you are used to eating chocolates daily, then you can change that habit by saying this to yourself, that when you feel like eating chocolate, then eat the vegetable snack first then chocolate later. You will be building your habits by replacing the bad ones with the good habit. For the new habits to survive, you will need repetition so that they can stick to your mind. Below is the list of the good habits that can be picked by individuals and if they implement them, then they will transform their habits and life completely.

## Waking up Early

Waking up early will increase productivity because it contributes greatly to the accomplishment of the goals but also brings balance in their lives. You will only get up early if you had enough sleep. This can be achieved if you get to bed early or at a reasonable time and wake up early. You will enjoy life and see the benefits of greater concentrations. You will concentrate if you had enough sleep.

## Be Ready to Learn

 Be that person who will be curious to know something, and above all, will be willing to learn that particular thing. If this will continue, then you are going to be a great person sooner than later. Developing the habit of exploring new habits and strengthening existing knowledge can bring a great improvement in your life. What it takes to accomplish all this is the urge to be ready to learn, and you will be boosting your learning curve. Doing this will not take much of your time if you will be more than willing.

## Setting Priorities

You have several tasks, and you are trying to tackle them at the same time, will you succeed in handling all the tasks? The answer is no, and you need to prioritize the responsibility. Try to see which one has to be done with urgency. It is also good to prioritize your leisure activities and your goals. For example, watching television is of lesser priority than accomplishing tasks that will contribute to your goal. Don't prioritize things that don't contribute to your goals. If they don't add value to your life and goal, exclude them in your priorities.

## Have Resilience

This will be of great help if stricken by disaster, you easily step up and try to reorganize things before you lose everything. You will have built your mind in a way that it will cope easily and find a solution to the problem you will be encountering. The only way to strengthen resilience is by believing in your abilities. When faced with tribulations, don't give up, but you should keep moving. Move out of a problem by re-organizing things one by one.

## Being Grateful

This is a powerful habit if inculcated in our lives at a tender age. Then we can go far with everything we undertake. If you are a position to be thankful even when something small is done to you, then you will break free the hard times as well. You will appreciate what life has offered. Being grateful brings one joy and happiness because you have meaning in whatever you have achieved in terms of material things. When you are grateful, you become content with what you have.

## Motivating Yourself

If you have the habit of motivating yourself whenever you accomplish anything, then forever, that habit will be part of you. This habit will be instilled by yourself. No one else can ignite such a habit in your own life. People may try and motivate you, but with time, you will find that they got tired on the way. You can look for effective ways to do motivation. Keep practicing it each day so that you will keep the fire burning.

## Be Positive

The way to think can either build you or destroy your life. if you are that person who will always think of failure, then it will happen. You will find that in everything that you try doing then failure becomes part of instead of success. Having positive thinking will act as fuel to your problem. No matter how hard it can be to find a solution to your problem but the positivity you will easily find a solution to the challenge. Being positive has an impact on your life and health. It will help one to live a life with no stress at all.

**Have a Vision**

Are you that person who sees himself or herself succeeding in one way or the other? If you visualize yourself, then it can give positive results. By having a positive vision, then the brain will help you to look into steps in which you will take so that you can accomplish. The main reason why visualization is important is that the mind will be used, and it is hard for the mind to differentiate reality from what it has set to accomplish.

**Setting Goals**

Do you have goals in life? a life without a goal is like going hiking without a map. You will be wandering in the forest, but you will not have the right route out of the forest. Same case in life, no set goals, then no direction in life. You will be wandering doing other things but, in the end, it will not add value to your life. a goal gives you direction, gives the necessary focus to overcome the necessary obstacles in life. You can do this by writing your goals down, then make it a habit of reviewing them daily.

**Have Room for Improvement**

It gets to some point in life when you get to abandon the old way and get to create some room for something new. The rule does not only limit us to the old ways but something that will bring a difference to our achievements. It got to bring positive achievement. By doing that, you are creating room for improvement and letting go of things that don't add value.

## Make and Meet the Decisions

The decisions you make can either build or destroy. Be careful when it comes to deciding because the moment they are made, no reverse gear. If planning to change the decision, it may cost you a lot of things. Your success depends greatly on the decision you make. To some other individuals, they spend more time overthinking a problem. By doing that, they will be wasting time on one problem. People don't want to make the wrong decision; that is the reason they will take long before making one. They don't know that deciding whether right or wrong is much better than not making one. Instead of wasting time and you are there, marking your plan and remarking. Act upon what you have at that particular time and will only make adjustments as you move instead of letting indecision to kill your productivity.

## Meditation

If you want to change many aspects of your life, then you should start meditating on what you are planning to change. This habit has not been valued by many, and the reason are they see it as a useless habit that cannot help one. In the real sense, this is the habit in which it relieves stress and at the same time, will reduce depression. Those who fear to think, then this can be the best habit for them.

## Do Physical Exercise

When you have regular activities, then you are on the right track of living a healthy life. Regular exercise improves your mental health. By doing regular exercises, then you will be boosting your energy and your mood as well. Once you have, it has a habit, and then you will never be tempted to push it to the next day.

## Have Little Breaks in Life

We have become so busy with life, and we forget to enjoy the little breaks that we get. Nowadays we spend more time on social media forgetting that is depriving us of the times having leisure time. We have many distracters, but if we can slot in time for taking a break, then it will become a habit. At your break, lean back, relax and don't do anything that should take a couple of minutes. The little breaks are effective because, after the break, you will feel refreshed.

## Make New Friends

When it becomes a habit of meeting someone new every day, it can refresh your mind. You will end up having a different discussion from what you had the previous day. The different people you will meet will challenge you in different ways. From that, you will be built in all aspects. What is important of all is that you get to meet the right kind of people who will share their private lives stories and professional stories as well. Such people can be a blessing to you.

## Learn from Those Who Have Made It

When you meet up with new people, you will be able to learn new things from them. It may be hard to meet with those who are experts in a particular field. But you will find that some have written books, others have blog or documentations. Knowing the lives of these experts will act as inspiration on your side. You get to know how they achieved in life, and this will motivate you to do more than what they accomplished.

## Listening to Others

It is great when people pay attention when you are talking, it is a sign of respect, and it means that you are following what you are saying. But nowadays, what has happened to our conversations? We have people who like to dominate in a conversation. At that particular time, you will find that those who were listening are now thinking about how they will get that chance to also conveyor say whatever idea they may be having. We should be ready to listen to others because by doing that, we will be improving the relationship. It also helps us to be a better negotiator.

## Eating Healthy

This is a habit which has been used badly by people, more so the lazy ones who run for fast food instead of cooking a healthy meal and eating it. When you have too much work, then you fail to take a well-balanced meal, you making it difficult for your body. By eating healthy, you will be building a foundation of living a happy life.

In conclusion, it can be hard to have new habits.

You will have many challenges in that journey as you try and getting new habits. At some point in life, you will find that old habits will keep appearing. That should not be the reason for giving up because of the challenges. You should be patient and stick to the new behavior you have acquired for a longer time. After that, you will cross the line, and the new habit will be part of you, and you will engage in it automatically.

# Chapter 12: Practical Ways to Use Emotional Intelligence

Self-management and relationship management serve great importance here. Stop, pause for a moment, and assess your situation. Examine where you are in your life, and what you plan to do next. If you are in a committed relationship, think about how your actions can affect your partner. Carefully consider what you do or say to accurately gauge where the relationship goes.

This also applies to the workplace. You are at work and have a project due by the end of the day. You are tirelessly working on that project, but more rush projects show up on the docket. This upsets you, only because it seems to not end and you have a lot on your shoulders. You grow weary and tired, wondering if your efforts are even being appreciated. You resent your employers. This is where you have to put your emotional intelligence to good use.

Pause for a moment and take a deep breath. Getting upset about your current situation will not help you in the least. It might make your performance worse. Remember, you want to make good decisions logically, especially in the workplace. In this setting, take a moment to look at the number of projects you have on your docket. Take them down one at a time. We are all

112

human beings, so we have to go at the pace we are used to. Because of this, we have to know our limits. It is not the end of the world if you cannot get to every project in time. Ask for help if you need it. We all need help and sometimes we resist the urge to ask for it. Doing this will also improve your relationships with people. When asked for help, many people would jump at the chance to assist someone. It is human nature to want to help your fellow humans. But one thing we have not gone over yet is how we use emotional intelligence to test our health.

Ever visit the doctor? It is not fun. You are constantly worrying about what might be wrong with you, and you really do not want to know. It is terrifying and it can be costly. That is the number one reason people avoid the doctor's office. But your health is important. People with strong emotional intelligence realize this, but do not always act on it. As exemplified before, empaths care more about helping others and it can often come at the detriment of their well-being. Because of this, establishing communication is important in matters of health. People often like to hide their health woes from close family and friends for fear of gaining too much sympathy. They do not want things to change and do not want to risk upsetting the status quo. This can be dangerous, especially if a close relative being there could be of some comfort to you.

Instead, resist the urge to act like this. Your emotional intelligence should tell you that others are capable of empathy, and you need not hide the horrors of your life to maintain order. Trust is important in any relationship and you need to establish trust not just in the good times, but the bad times as well. You do not just have to trust yourself, but others. People who do not trust others lead a cycle of behavior that is unhealthy. For example, imagine you suffered a tragedy at a young age. You are eight years old and your parents have both passed away. The only person left in your life is your uncle, who has agreed to take care of you. But there is still a huge void in your life. Your parents passed away and you have to find a way, at a young age, to move on. You can still establish healthy emotional intelligence despite the circumstances. A person could rise to the challenge and overcome any obstacles that life put in their way. An unhealthy pattern would be if you were to stop trusting the world after this tragedy occurred. Do not close yourself off from the world and allow yourself to lose faith in everyone and everything. Instead, learn to allow other people into your inner circle. Give people a chance to make an impression on you and form that trust that you lost a long time ago. We can build emotional intelligence over a lifespan, with never-ending opportunities for growth.

## Communicating and Dealing with Your Feelings

So how do we communicate and deal with our feelings? It is a never-ending battle with the feelings we feel every day. We could wake up feeling amazing and wanting to conquer the world one day. The next day, we could feel miserable and not want to get out of bed. For most people, there is no consistency in our feelings and what will happen next. This is normal and part of what being a human being is all about. You must be ready to accept this and realize that not every day will be perfect. There will be days when you feel terrible and feel utter sadness. The sadness and desolation can feel like the worst feelings in the world. They can consume you if you let them and you must be careful to avoid going down that dark path. Try not to overthink everything and keep it simple.

One thing we have not talked about is feeling suppression. There is a delicate balance here. You do not want to overstep someone and be aggressive. You do not want to suppress how you are feeling all the time. If you do that, eventually, you will burst and probably go off on a rampage. Both situations are unhealthy and not productive. You need to find a balance. Find a balance that fits both angles and try to come to an understanding that will be beneficial to everyone. Your feelings are just as important as others. Just because you are sensitive to others, it does not mean you have to ignore your desires. If you do this, you will never be happy. Happiness is always the goal, and to achieve that you need to maintain and keep improving upon your emotional intelligence. It needs to be a repetitive thing that never stops. There needs to be a constant effort on your part to keep picking yourself up and never letting up.

This is where you have to stop and think about the bigger picture. Think about how the emotions you feel are impacting your life and decide whether it is worth letting them do so.

Let me explain. You are driving in traffic. The people in front of you are driving terribly. They are driving like the worst drivers on earth. They are slow and indecisive. These drivers cut you off and are going 20 miles below the speed limit. You wonder how can people drive this badly and how can they get a license? You do not realize it, but your emotions are rising. Your anger is getting bigger and bigger and eventually it will consume you. Basically, you are letting people you don't even know ruin your day.

Stop and think about this for a moment. You are getting upset because you may be in a rush. Or you may not be in a rush and simply want to get to where you are going. These drivers are a hindrance to you and it is ruining your peace of mind. Consider whether this is worth it. Figure out why these drivers are upsetting you and process it from there. Take a moment to figure out if getting upset about this is really the best course of action. It does not solve your current problem. The drivers will still drive badly, and there is nothing you can do about it. Sure, you can always yell at the other drivers. There is that option. However, there may be consequences to doing that. The other drivers may think you are nuts and call the cops on you. Or, you may find a nuts driver and it can endanger your life. All of this is over traffic. You let your anger get the best of you and it could hurt you. Take a moment and consider if it is worth it. Is it worth it? Would you let people you don't even know upset you that easily? It is just a drive. Everyone has somewhere to go and people all drive at their speed. It is best to go out and just take this in without letting it upset you.

You can do this by understanding your emotional triggers. What upsets you? Do you know what upsets you easily? It may not be easy to determine. We all get angry at different things. Anger is a normal human reaction. We are not advocating suppressing all your anger. If you do this, you will burst. We are merely advocating finding measures to limit your anger and control how it affects you and others. There are many forms of emotional triggers that we have. It is all different for everyone. For example, some people get emotionally triggered when someone breaks off a relationship with them. It can come as a shock to the system. Someone you adored no longer can stand the sight of you. They do not want to be around you as much as you want to be around them. It hurts, it really hurts. It is a feeling that you cannot control. You feel a mix of anger and sadness. This is because often it is unexpected and you did not see it coming. Because you did not expect this, it stings you a little deeper.

But what if you were never with them to begin with? It is hurtful to get rejected by someone you have an interest in. You have

117

built this ideal and worked the courage to approach this person with interest, only for them to tell you they have no interest. They are not into you and have communicated that there is no chance for you. This applies to not getting that job you wanted, too. A human resources manager rejects you for a job you had hopes of getting. Because of this, it reflects upon your self-confidence. You take a hit, wondering where it all went wrong.

You can also get emotionally triggered because of helplessness. This can be because of a situation outside your power and control. Because it is outside your control, it frustrates you and this can cause you to get upset at the situation. You dislike not having control. It triggers you and you want to make a change. But you soon learn that you cannot. It is too late and you are powerless.

Being ignored can trigger you. It can frustrate you because you feel like nothing. Many people would rather accept rejection than have someone ignore them. Getting ignored implies that you are not even worthy of a response. This is the feeling that many job seekers feel when they apply for a job and do not hear a word. It is also the feeling that they feel when they interview and do not hear any feedback. This is like a situation where you are being ignored by your friends or a significant other. It is not the best thing in the world.

When someone disapproves of something you do, that can be equally frustrating. You can feel the disappointment resonate within your body. It can be something as simple as a parent asking you why you do something that you do. Or, it could be a friend criticizing something you do. We dislike disappointing people, and we dislike when others give us disapproving looks.

It is worse when someone blames you for something. Whether you did something or not, someone pointing a finger at you can cause your emotional triggers to explode. You feel anger and resentment and the first instinct is to defend yourself. Why would you not? You are being accused of something and you feel like the world is against you.

What about when someone is too busy for you? We have all heard that story. You want to hang out with your friends, but they seem to always be busy. They seem to never spend any time with you. This makes you question your validity, and how much you mean to them. It can be an emotional trigger if you let it, and it can be harmful.

That can be equally frustrating if you are visiting someone and they do not appear to be happy to see you. We like to assume that when we spend time with someone, that they are enjoying our company as much as we enjoy theirs. That is not always the case, however. Remember, in life, not everyone will like you. Sometimes, people do not want to see you. It is not always your fault. Occasionally, that is just how it works. Some people will be happier to see you than others. This can also work in reverse. Some people will be too excited to see you.

Someone might have an interest in you and come onto you in a needy way. This is something you do not expect, and it takes you by surprise. You felt sadness for the person and the way they feel for you. This encounter may even creep you out a little and you can become uncomfortable. This feeling of discomfort can impact how you interact with the person from that point forward and change your outlook on them.

This also applies when you are in a relationship with someone. Whether it is a significant other, a friend, or relative, someone trying to control you can hurt you. This is because you dislike other people telling you what to do or how to act. It can trigger an automatic response of defensiveness. Your defense mechanisms go into overdrive and you seek the fastest way out of the situation. Sometimes, there are no simple solutions and you have to face the obstacles you are dealing with at the moment.

These emotional triggers have the same thing in common. They are all feelings that can either overtake you or can be managed. It all depends on how you respond to every situation. Only when you change your response can you truly evolve and manage your emotional intelligence.

This is where you have to find healthy alternatives to the emotional triggers that ache you. Go around your obstacles and set a precedent for what you plan to do next. You need to find solutions to your problems in the most productive ways possible to ensure that you can successfully manage your emotions. The first step here is eliminating all the negativity in your life.

## Controlling Negative Emotions

Negativity is an inevitable thing. We all experience negative emotions in our lives. It is a normal thing to experience negativity. Negativity can come in the form of anger, sadness, resentment, or frustration.

We could get angry at our current situation and vent to anyone willing to listen. Our sadness comes from not being able to accomplish what we want in the grand scope of things. We resent the world for allowing us to struggle. The frustration stems from the fact that we are struggling. Again, these emotions are normal.

However, it is not normal to let these emotions consume you. To lead a successful life, you must control the negativity going on in your life. It is not just about external situations; it is about internal thought processes. We are our own worst enemy, but we could also be our greatest champion. You need to learn to balance the negative energy that is surrounding you and use it to your advantage. How do you do this?

Start by overcoming all the negative thoughts you have about yourself and your life. If you have failed at something today, convince yourself you will succeed tomorrow. Sports are the best analogy for this. A professional football team can have a bad season and be terrible. They can win only three games and lose 13 in a single season. Because of this, a lot of negativity can rise and the organization can get discouraged. However, the best course of action is for that team to realize that there are better days ahead. They can focus on their positives and try to improve on the negatives. That way, when they play next season, they can achieve more victories. Failure today is not the end of the world. We all fail at something. It is what helps us grow. We achieve more when we have struggled to do it before. You can learn a lot from losing. It teaches us the value of working hard and gives you the ability to realize your limits. Failing can devastate but overcoming failure can be uplifting and wonderful. There are many success stories in the world of people who overcame the odds. Those stories are proof that anyone can achieve anything if they put their minds to it. Not succeeding at something does not have to be the end of the story. It can be the start of how you overcome the negativity and achieve beyond your wildest dreams.

# Chapter 13 : Strategies to Reduce Stress and Curb Anxiety

Exercise is a vital tool for managing worry. When you exercise, brain chemicals are released that counteract low moods, worry and anxiety. Exercise also acts as a distraction from worries and reduces nervousness. Exercise at least once a day for half an hour, with cardio exercises at least three days a week.

Incorporate organized problem-solving strategies to handle stressors that contribute to your worry. When challenged with a difficult situation or life problem, most people often don't know how to handle these difficulties and lack enough coping skills; they feel as if they're incapable of controlling what they're faced with. Such feelings cause people to worry.

Everyone has problems and challenges in their lives, but they are more visible and difficult to handle if you always get worried. A useful strategy to combat this is training in organized problem-solving. Efficient problem- solving techniques minimize, reduce, control and even prevent worrying in our daily lives.

Avoid activities and situations that foster anxiety by confronting your fears and facing them directly but gradually. For instance, you could place them in a hierarchy, depending on which step you fear the most. These fears could be:

1.      Arriving late for a meeting

2.      Not checking your mobile phone for one hour

3.      Going grocery shopping without a shopping list

4.      Planning a birthday party

5.      Accepting an invitation without checking with your calendar

6.      Going out without your mobile phone for the day

## Adopt Cognitive Interventions

There are two errors that those who have GAD tend to make:

Overestimation: They are always on edge, overestimating the likelihood of catastrophe. For example, they think thoughts like:

"This will be a disaster!" or "I had better prepare for the worst scenario".

Underestimation: They are often underestimating their ability to cope with their problems. For instance, they might think thoughts like, "I will have a breakdown." or "I won't be capable of dealing with this situation".

If you have a problem with thoughts like these, what can you do? Simple! Challenge these negative thoughts by mastering how to recognize distressing thoughts and whether these thoughts are realistic.

For example, you may have to ask yourself what evidence you have to support these thoughts. If you can't find any, you may not need to dwell on it. Also, it might be that the best thing to do is to identify how likely it is that your fears for the future will come true.

Furthermore, folks with GAD should also continually work at challenging their beliefs and assumptions regarding themselves. For instance, a person's worry could be that he will never get prepared on time, and this might be followed up with the assumption that if things go wrong, he should be blamed and the creeping belief that he or she is a failure. Even though some believe that worry prevents harmful occurrences, this is inaccurate. Instead, it increases one's level of anxiety.

Well, as soon a person has been able to identify and question his or her negative thoughts, then the next line of action is shifting attention away from the negative thoughts. Cognitive Behavioral Therapy assists in identifying and challenging these assumptions and helping individuals to develop alternative beliefs that are healthier and better for their personal well-being. Experiences have shown that mindfulness-based interventions will also aid you to remain focused.

Adopt Emotion Regulation and Mindfulness

Recent studies have suggested that worry may present itself as a way of doing away with emotional processing. Involve yourself in what is called emotion-regulation strategies and mindfulness skills, as these will boost the form and manner in which you identify and experience underlying emotions.

Do away with the use of medications that will sedate you. Don't binge to relieve your anxiety. They may provide temporary relief from anxiety, but frankly, it will come back later. Instead of doing these, set up a time to consult a specialist or go for CBT if symptoms occur for longer than three months regardless of the above measures.

## Realistic Ways to Cope with Symptoms of Anxiety and Excessive Worrying

It's great to learn tips and tricks that we can use to wrestle anxiety and excessive worry. Each time that you find yourself in an unpleasant situation, ask yourself these simple but effective questions.

• Is my worry reasonable?

• Will what I fear happen?

• How can I be sure that what I fear will happen?

• Could there be any other plausible explanation or outcome in my situation?

- Am I trying to predict things in the distant future that I am unable to do something about?

- If this worst-case scenario occurs, will it really be as bad as I think that it will be?

- Is it worth worrying about?

- How would someone else view my worry?

## What is the Effect of Thinking the Way That You Do?

What will be the effect of thinking the way that you are thinking right now? Do these thoughts make you feel empowered to solve the problem at hand or do they discourage you from believing in yourself and feeling capable of facing the problem at hand? Are there instances where your worries are valid? Yes! Sometimes we worry about things that are likely to happen. In this situation, what you will need to do is to face your worry and do something about it if you can.

If not, you may need to let it go. For those who are experts when it comes to worrying, this may seem impossible. However, you could say to yourself, "There is absolutely nothing that could be done to alter this right now". Then you can find some other activity to occupy your mind and distract you from this situation that you have no control over.

## Is There a True Problem to Solve?

If there really is a problem to solve, then you might have to focus your attention on a practical solution for it. In this case, you might turn to problem-solving skills to deal head-on with the things that are worrying you.

Below are six structured problem-solving techniques that you can use to do this:

1.      Write down precisely what you think the real problem is.

2.      Write down all the possible solutions that you could think of; don't eliminate the bad ones yet.

3.      Consider each solution carefully and logically.

4.      Select the most practical solution.

5.      Plan carefully how you will work on that solution.

6.      Do it.

**Note:** Anxiety is not your fault. Daily life and comes with stressors that can affect a person's thoughts, feelings, and everyday functioning!

## 10 Things That You Might Not Realize Can Be Signs of Anxiety

It is normal to worry. Everyone is worried at one time or another, most often with discernment. After all, being aware of possible dangers leads us to take logical actions, such as paying attention before crossing a street! But it is certainly possible to worry too much.

If, one day, someone discovers a lump in his/her throat, one will most certainly be worried. We will feel panic, discomfort, and anxiety; we may decide to react, to search the internet for information, to make an appointment with a doctor, and to subject ourselves to a multitude of exams to know what it is. Our thoughts race: What if it's cancer? What if there is no treatment? Will we die? As we catastrophize, we are already experiencing a disaster, with all the physical and psychological impressions of anxiety associated with it, which leaves us feeling tired and demoralized.

In the first situation, our anxiety remains productive. Founded on something concrete — there is a ball that could affect our lives — it helps us make decisions, solve hardships, and deal with danger. In the second case, anxiety paralyzes us. Often, we worry without effectively setting up guidelines to solve the problem.

Are you convinced that worrying is an ingrained feature of your personality? That worrying about your financial situation, your health, the health of others, your work, your family, your friends, your safety, crime, etc. is altruism? That by considering the worst, you preserve yourself?

Here are some signs that indicate that you are anxious:

You're always busy, but you can never seem to get things done.

If you are unable to complete a job or perform a task as planned, you panic, and you constantly seek reassurance and reassurance.

## Catastrophic existential thoughts plague you

You always expect the worst. For example, your spouse is late. He was at a meeting that may have been run late, but the worst scenarios haunt you. You are convinced that he has been in some sort of accident, has contracted a possible illness, or some other calamity has occurred.

## You're easily startled

In a situation where you are startled easily, there is a need to become more aware of your emotions. Research has established that if you are anxious, you have an increased level of being startled by everyday occurrences, such as a door slamming or a car backing up.

## Your stomach is upset, but your doctor can't figure out why

If you constantly begin to have stomach problems, and have eliminated food poisoning and other stomach illnesses, your stomach upset could be the result of anxiety. You can become sick to your stomach due to anxiety.

## You're a perfectionist

Although being a perfectionist is not a worrisome thing, the inability to go outside your comfort zone to avoid mistakes can be a sign of anxiety. If, when you venture outside your comfort zone, you don't achieve what you want, and you begin to feel ashamed and inferior, this is a sign of anxiety due to perfectionism.

It has been pointed out by experts that perfectionists tend to reject help, even when they are worried that they may fail.

## Everyone around you is getting on your nerves

It is important to relax after a long day. Anxiety often prevents you from doing so. At this point, you may become easily irritated at any action from your friends or relatives. If you feel like this, the possibility that you are feeling anxious is very high.

When you feel uneasy or anxious, look for a physical activity that you like to do or something else to distract your mind.

## You are incapable of making decisions

Another sign of anxiety is the emotional attachment becoming too overwhelmed to make decisions. You get bogged down when considering the possible consequences of your decision, and you get stuck in between several different choices.

## You cannot sleep

Anxiety often disturbs our sleep, which is one of the most important things necessary to stay healthy. Without a night of good sleep, we put our health and our life in danger. For example, driving while we are sleep-deprived becomes as dangerous as when we drive after drinking alcohol.

You may become very restless in many cases and suffer because of increasing sleep disorders.

## You're having random chills or hot flashes

In a situation where you begin to suffer from chills and hot flashes without being sick, it can be as a result of anxiety. You should consult your doctor to understand the concept of generalized anxiety disorder.

Also, when you have nightmares and flashbacks, which remind those affected of the traumatic experiences and trigger traumatic memories that would otherwise have long been forgotten, these are signs of anxiety.

## You feel like you have failed at life

Perhaps the worst feeling that can show that you are worried is when you begin to feel like you are not good enough for the world. You begin to feel useless to your loved ones and even at work. If you are constantly feeling this way, then you are likely to have an anxiety disorder.

# Chapter 14: How to Make Better Decisions in Your Life

How often do you make decisions? Every day. No matter what we answer, though, that's the reality! We are always compelled to make decisions, though the nature of our decisions differs greatly. For example, there are big decisions and small decisions. Small decisions shouldn't take much time; big ones may take days or even weeks. And yet, we can't avoid it; we must make those decisions. However, before any decision is made, one must consider some essential factors.

Indecisiveness is a negative trait that could slow down the entire decision-making process. Most people aren't proud of the fact that they are indecisive. An indecisive person might pressure others to decide for them, either indirectly or directly.

For these people, making choices themselves can be a scary thing since they will keep asking themselves: What would eventually happen if I make a bad decision? It's normal to be fearful when you are making the decision yourself, but know that as you continue to do this, you will trust yourself more, and you will practice the act of making big decisions.

And the more you keep making significant decisions yourself, the more you will be glad to exclude other people from the decision-making process; you will need their approval less.

Therefore, since the basic idea is to make decisions yourself, independent of anyone, the following tips will help you to make decisions easily and more quickly. Consider the following six methods:

## Be Aware of What You Want

One of the ways to identify what you want is to determine what your goals are. When you become more aware of what you want in life, and when you decide what your goals will be, it is evident that you will be able to make better choices. David Welch, a political science professor whose work was published in the Huffington Post, says that people who aren't self-reflective will undeniably end up making bad decisions because they aren't aware of what they want in life in the first place.

Therefore, when making a decision, you should ask yourself where you want to be next year and if that decision will help to take you where you want to go. If your answers are quite different from what you are working towards, then the best thing to do is to make a different decision. So, the critical point here is to identify what you want in life.

## Ask for Advice, but Make Your Own Choices

Admittedly, making a decision doesn't mean that you should not seek advice from others; after all, no one is an island of knowledge. But you should be cautious; this could be a decision regarding your relationship, your well-being, or your job. Do you feel comfortable confiding in others and asking for their advice?

Others may not understand exactly how you feel, but should that be a reason why you shouldn't seek advice? No! You can gather information from them and make your final decision yourself. It is also important to remember that you are ultimately the one who will have to live with your decision.

## Pay Attention to Your Gut

Yes, we all know ourselves better than we realize. But in some cases, most people ignore the message that their gut is telling them since they don't want to hear the consequences their decision will bring or deal with the reality of it. It is essential to be objective and clear-headed each time we are faced with some difficult choices, such as making big decisions.

Therefore, when you are making a tough decision, it's ideal to write down everything you are thinking and the reason you think you are feeling that way. As you begin to have an internal dialogue with yourself, you may become lost in an endless maze of thoughts. By writing down your thoughts, you will strengthen your conviction and are more likely to listen to your gut.

## Ensure That You Are in the Right State of Mind

A person who isn't in a good mood will find it tougher to make the right decision. Unpleasant feelings that could influence the decision-making process include stress, hunger, and drowsiness.

Take, for instance, if you are trying to figure out what you will eat for lunch when you are hungry, how easily will you be able to decide? And this is a relatively small decision.

Therefore, to avoid being rash, when making a big decision, you should ensure that you are feeling comfortable and emotionally balanced. Then, after these criteria have been met, make your decision.

## Learn to Trust Yourself

Don't confuse trusting yourself with arrogance and having a big ego. Experts have said that the first person an individual has to trust is himself/herself. Just because you believe in yourself doesn't make you arrogant and proud.

No one could be as consistently supportive of you in the same way that you will learn to be. Then how do you accomplish trusting yourself? Be kind to yourself; when you do, it boosts your self-confidence, and you will not need to seek approval from other people before you make any decision.

Trusting yourself, too, will let you make a sound decision eventually, even after meeting people for advice. Also, when you love and care for yourself, your connection with others becomes strengthened. Don't forget that it's a task to have the strength to trust yourself. So, as soon as confidence is met, then you will be pushed and thus be courageous to make big decisions in the future.

## Practice, Practice, Practice

The way you get improve is by making your own decisions every day. If it becomes part of your day-to-day routine, you will have more confidence in decision-making and taking inspired action will get easier and faster.

According to psychologists, mastering the process of making the right decisions is depends on a lot of factors. They include a person's developmental age or stage, their idea of what's right and wrong, and their understanding of what the decision-making process entails.

Since you are unfamiliar with making big decisions for yourself, try it for a week, and don't ask anyone else to make your decisions for you. As you gradually improve, then it will become part of you, and thus you will be in control, without the influence of another person.

With these six tips, what's the bottom line? To be good at making big decisions, you really must devote a lot of time and practice. And the moment you are there, you are your boss.

## How to Stop Expecting the Worst

Have you ever thought about what keeps our brain from behaving logically? It's fear! Why? It's because fear looks so real and essential that if we dare ignore it, something terrible might happen. And that's exactly the scenario that occurs when you are expecting the worst. You are trying all you can, but it's just resulting in a magnification of your fear, anxiety, and stress.

Here is an anecdote that will explain this phenomenon further. One man said: Generally, he usually looks at his rearview mirror many times before he gets home. He knows that it's not the best thing to do, but he said he thinks doing that is the best way to be conscious and know if someone is tailgating him, and he mentions that it annoys him to see people following him.

So, one night, as he was driving home, he notices that a car is following him closely; the vehicle keeps in close contact with him, following in him every direction he goes. And after making a few turns, he started to get suspicious and asked himself: Is this person following him? Was he seen entering his car? Could they be a serial killer? Is he their next victim? Many questions were flowing, but he couldn't answer them. Maybe he's watched too many true crime shows?

He convinced himself to think positively and think of ways that he could resolve his situation. He could drive past his house so that he could fool them to disallow them from knowing where he resides. To him, it seemed like a good plan. Then something happened next.

After his next turn, he noticed that they went in a different direction; he kept going, and nothing showed up. At that time, he realized that they weren't following him anymore. What did he do next? He breathed a sigh of relief, and now he felt that it was ridiculous for him to think that they were following him.

In the real sense, that is what happens when you are anticipating or expecting the worst. At that stage, your body starts to panic; you breathe faster, your heartbeat quickens, and you start to breathe more shallowly. You will start to picture horrific scenarios in your head and alter your behavior as a result of that fear.

What happens to you during this period will affect your mood and stress level, and negatively impact your ability to make good decisions. So, how do you stop expecting the worst? Let's expand on these four points sequentially.

## 1. Identify Your Fears

First, you have to ask yourself: When you are always expecting the worst? Are those times when you deliver a presentation at work, when you are writing an exam, when you are keenly worried about your loved one's safety or your own, or when you are participating in social interactions? Yes, many things could make you fearful; identify them.

When you determine some specific scenarios, then you will have a higher tendency to identify where your fears lie and what your beliefs are about certain situations. The more you can be aware of what triggers your anxiety, thus making you expect the worst, the more that you will have the strength and power to stop it. So, don't hesitate to take a moment to reflect on when you are usually expecting the worst and why you are doing so.

If you have generalized anxiety, you likely expect the worst-case scenario. In that case, you are always anxious, overwhelmed, and stressed, and your heightened arousal will affect your thinking; you are more likely to overestimate adverse outcomes. Here are a few questions to ponder:

Reflection Questions:

- When do I expect the worst?

- How do these affect my emotions, thoughts, behaviors?

## 2. Challenge Your Expectations

Of course, when you expect the worst, your mind will always tend to create unreasonable and unrealistic scenarios. Honestly, we're blessed with the ability to imagine; it inspires wonder and creativity. The downside is that when we expect the worst, we don't always consider the facts of the situation and relative probabilities of all possible outcomes.

So, when imagining an adverse event, our fear could become so all-consuming that we will neglect the facts and fail to look at the reality. This is normal, though. But we mustn't forget that this comes from our basic need and desire for survival. To preserve our safety, we are inclined to overestimate the tendency that bad things will happen.

Take, for example, many people who are afraid of flying. When I flew on an airplane recently, we had some turbulence, and a woman who was sitting next to me was nervous and held onto the chair that was in front of her due to fear. Like her, many other people were worried. And it's understandable; whatever happens in an airplane is definitely not in your locus of control.

However, the odds of dying in a plane crash are 1 in 11 million. You are far more likely to be either hit by lighting or be severely attacked by a shark than you will die in a plane crash. How does that make you feel? So, these facts could correctly be used to challenge the logic behind your fear.

### 3. Get Your Feelings Out

Emotions and thoughts can be so toxic if you have no outlet. Therefore, it is very advisable to journal and use other artistic methods to process your emotions in the right way, and that will help you to feel better.

So, write down your thoughts in a journal so you can speed up your recovery. Don't keep anything inside just because you would feel embarrassed if someone else were to read it. Also, you may speak with a trusted confidant if you would feel more comfortable doing so.

### 4. Take Control

To take control, you need to begin with what you have control over. As difficult as it may be to do so, it is important to let the rest go. When you sit and ponder the worst-case scenario, you are not helping yourself. So, pay attention only to things you can do.

There are lots of things that you can't control; a list will assist you in clarifying them in more detail. Here are two important ones:

- What other people feel, do, or think about you.
- Situations that you have no control over.

Thus, when you focus on what you can do, you will boost your confidence level, and there will also be a decrease in your stress level; you will be able to take confident action when and where it is necessary, without overthinking.

The following four points highlight some of the best reasons why you should be able to stop expecting the worst-case scenario.

## Worrying Does Not Solve Problems

Worrying does not provide you with any benefits, nor does it solve any of your problems. Don't fool yourself by thinking that the more you worry about a situation, the more you will work toward achieving it.

When you do, you are only making yourself unnecessarily stressed, tense, and anxious, which negatively will impact your ability to think critically. Therefore, each time you think about the worst-case scenario, ask yourself: Is this really helping me? It does not, and this is the first important step to mastering your thoughts, reducing your overthinking and anxiety, and improving your life.

# Chapter 15 : The Nervous System

As I promised in the Chapter 3, I'm going to tell you more about the vagus nerve, his functions and how it is correlated to Overthinking and other behavioral disorders strictly related to overthinking, such as anxiety.

This chapter is going to serve as your basic guide to understanding the nervous system, how it works, and the way that we commonly divide it up to understand it. When you read through this chapter, you will be learning all about how the body functions, but in terms that are easily understood. You do not need to have much background knowledge at all to be able to understand what you will be walked through during this chapter.

## Understanding Nerves and their Functions

Firstly, we must go over the nerves themselves. Nerves are bundles of neurons—they allow you to transfer information from one place to another. Generally speaking, one nerve is made up of many neurons, which connect closely together. The nerves act by sending electrochemical impulses, passing the message from nerve to nerve across the body.

This electrochemical impulse is like a series of chain reactions in which one impulse is translated down the chain. Let's imagine, for example, that you have just touched a cold drink. Your hand touches the cold surface, and the cold immediately activates those neurons at the surface of your hand. These neurons activate and send the message for "COLD!" down them. It is firstly transmitted via electrical connection down the axon of the individual neuron, at which point the message eventually arrives at the axon terminals—the ending receptors that reach out to connect to other neurons. Each neuron has many different terminals, and some can have hundreds. At this point, the electrical impulse cannot continue on its own. The axon terminals then take that electrical impulse and translate it into a chemical message for the next neuron. The chemicals are then passed from the first neuron to the next one, allowing for the activation and therefore transmission, of the message. The next neuron then repeats this message, over and over again, until it reaches the destination: The brain. Every neuron along the way essentially receives the message of "COLD!" and passes it along to the next one, much like how children may play telephone with a message.

This happens nearly instantaneously in most circumstances. The speeds of the neurons are usually fast enough that you do not notice the delay, nor do you realize that the message has been passed repeatedly from place to place before getting to the brain for processing—it simply seems automatic and fluid, and this is what the body seeks to do. The body wants everything to be nearly instantaneous because, at the end of the day, you need to be able to respond in an instant if you want to survive, which is the body's ultimate goal. The body wants to ensure that you survive long enough to propagate, and if you are not capable of doing so, you will most likely get eaten or killed at some point just due to not being responsive enough to survive.

Essentially, your nerves exist to be built up of countless neurons, allowing for direct communication to be facilitated. Neurons are like the building blocks for the neuron itself and allow for the functionality that you need. The neurons will also build up your brain, creating trillions of synapses. Those synapses are the connections that can be propagated from neuron to neuron to spread information.

## Understanding the Nervous System

Understanding the nervous system does not need to be difficult, however. If you can imagine it like a bunch of messengers that are all trying to send and receive messages, you have the gist of it. Essentially, everything that makes you who you are gets transmitted in some sort of message. You transmit these messages with ease, thanks to the nervous system that travels throughout the vast majority of your body. Even areas that you cannot actively feel are innervated so they can be regulated and function properly. Without this sort of regulation from the nervous system, these parts of the body would simply fail to work properly.

Your nervous system works primarily by having the brain work as a processor, though the spinal cord is also capable of some degree of processing power itself. The central nervous system will be comprised of the brain and spinal cord. The rest of the body is referred to as the peripheral nervous system—this is the webbing of nerves that exist outside of the central nervous system.

The peripheral nervous system becomes divided into two functions as well—it can be somatic when it is capable of being voluntarily controlled, or it can be autonomic when it is automatic. The peripheral nervous system divided in this manner will allow you to differentiate between the functions of the rest of the nervous system.

Your autonomic nervous system can be broken down even further. It can be thought of as sympathetic or parasympathetic. These refer to the response to the external world then. Sympathetic nervous system activation creates a stress response for the most part, while the parasympathetic nervous system is the calming response.

**Central Nervous System**

We will first start out by describing the central nervous system and its primary functions. This part of your nervous system is dedicated entirely to processing and regulation. You have the brain and the spinal cord responsible for this area of the nervous system. By and large, all of the heavy-duty work is done by the brain. This is where proper processing tends to occur. Your brain is responsible for keeping your body in homeostasis, meaning that it keeps the body functioning to the proper level to assure health. It makes sure that the rest of the body is told what to do via the nerves.

Your spinal cord is protected largely by the spine, and it is meant to allow for communication between the brain and the body. The spinal cord is where the vast majority of your nerves met up with the central nervous system, and the spinal cord then sends the messages up to the brain and back down and out to the body. However, this can also take care of reflexive movements, such as pulling away from something hot or painful to touch.

**Peripheral Nervous System**

As mentioned, the peripheral nervous system then becomes anything beyond the brain and spinal cord. Even your cranial nerves are technically peripheral to the central nervous system. This peripheral connection throughout the body is maintained by the constant web of neurons that go from place to place, creating new synapses, and therefore, paths that can be used to transmit data to the brain. Primarily, your peripheral nervous system is all about transmitting information rather than processing it. This nervous system is commonly broken down into either autonomic or somatic nervous systems.

## Autonomic Nervous System and the Vagus Nerve

The autonomic nervous system is the automatic part of your peripheral nervous system. That means that this is the area of the nervous system that is going to be actively regulating and controlling the body involuntarily. It is the areas of your nervous system that are involved in much of your organ's regulation as well as emotional and automatic responses. These are your instinctive reactions to stress, for example, which is primarily where the vagus nerve comes in.

This system is primarily divided into two—the sympathetic and the parasympathetic nervous systems. Each of these plays a special role in managing the body's response to their surroundings.

## The Sympathetic Nervous System

This is the default stress response for most people. It takes you into fight or flight mode—the mode in which you grow aggressive with your surroundings. You try to fight it off, or you try to flee. When you go into a sympathetic activation, you will find that your body is prepared to send money down toward the muscles to help propel them. The energy is directed here, so you will be capable of fending off a threat somehow. Think about it— if you are spending all of your energy digesting food, you will not be as effective as you should be in defending yourself. You need to be able to defend yourself to survive, but you can usually wait to digest your food until later on.

When you are in this particular activation, you will see a tendency toward higher heart rates, blood pressure, and respiratory rates to allow that energy to be redirected in the first place. Your body is entirely ready to fight, and you will likely see that you have the focus to do so. Your senses feel sharper, and your response time is quicker while your body prepares to do what it must to survive.

However, please note that when you are in this sort of activation for an extended time, you run the risk of anxiety and other issues due to the constant fluctuation of stress hormones within the body that are hazardous to your health. You want to avoid this at all costs.

**The Parasympathetic Nervous System**

The parasympathetic nervous system is like the other side of the autonomic coin. If the sympathetic nervous system is designed to energize and expend energy, the parasympathetic nervous system is all about shutting down and conserving energy. It is primarily considered to be the rest and digest system—it triggers your body to be in a state that will allow for the resting and digesting that you will need to better function. It will enable you to, for example, settle down and relax.

This is important to remember in other contexts as well. When you are in the parasympathetic activation, you are going to either be feeling like you are capable of being social, or you will feel like you are shutting down. Parasympathetic reflexes can leave you feeling calm and happy to eat and digest. It encourages social behaviors and will lead to an activation of the areas of the vagus nerve that are responsible for communication in general.

The parasympathetic nervous system becomes quite diverse in what it is capable of doing. It tells your body to slow down, so digestion can occur and makes you feel close enough to other people to be willing to socialize with them. It allows you to recognize and prioritize your need to slow down and relax. However, too much of it can lead to problems as well. When your parasympathetic nervous system goes into overdrive, you can wind up feeling subdued, depressed, or even find that you freeze up and dissociate. We will discuss this further later when discussing the anatomy of the vagus nerve in particular.

**The Vagus Nerve and the Autonomic Nervous System**

The vagus nerve controls this switch between sympathetic and parasympathetic functioning. It can override the sympathetic reactions, leading to a calming effect if it is activated strongly enough. It can choose to slow down enough to let that sympathetic nervous system kick into gear when necessary as well. Essentially, it becomes this sort of control switch that is capable of managing it all. It primarily takes care of this, allowing it to determine how you will respond to stress if you find that you are under stress in the first place, as well as recognizing how best to stop you from feeling it.

We will primarily be looking at the vagus nerve as this sort of regulator of stress responses throughout this book, as much of the dysfunction that you are likely to encounter throughout your life is going to be when you run into problems regulating that stress.

# Chapter 16 : Vagus Nerve

Every person has nerves. These are what make up the basics of an individual—they run through your body as information highways that allow you to not only recognize the world around you Your nerves within your bodywork to allow you to interact with the world—they provide you with sensory input that you can then process and then use to command the rest of your body. Essentially, the input is taken to the brain through your nerves. Your brain processes the information, and then sends the output to your body through those very same nerves. This is what allows you to navigate and interact with your environment and is integral to being you.

You have all sorts of nerves throughout your body. Some are for moving, and others are for sensing. They take input to the brain when they are afferent and they take output away from the brain when they are efferent. They allow you to be the person that you are, and therefore, are incredibly important. Without nerves, you cannot be the person that you are. You would not be sentient or able to do anything with your environment just by not being able to have that sophisticated system that you have now.

One particular nerve, however, is important to pay attention to. Your vagus nerve is a sort of wanderer—it originates in the brainstem and travels throughout your body. It goes through your neck and travels throughout your torso, innervating many different areas to allow them to function properly. We are going to be looking at the vagus nerve and how it works with the body. We are going to understand just how important the vagus nerve is and what it does.

**What is a Vagus Nerve?**

Your vagus nerve is a pair of nerves that travel from the brain and down into the torso. It is the largest of the cranial nerves, traveling to interact with the majority of your internal organs. The vagus nerve is responsible for your parasympathetic nervous system, in particular, making it a major part of the autonomic system within your body. Your autonomic nervous system keeps your body functioning properly and makes sure that everything that you do is particularly tailored to ensuring that you can survive in the world around you.

This primarily happens through emotions. Your vagus nerve, in particular, can cause you to calm down through the activation of the parasympathetic nervous system. This tells the body to stop and calm down somewhat to ensure that you are able to stop and digest rather than exist in fight or flight mode.

Your vagus nerve will begin at the back of your neck, connected to the brain at the brainstem. It leaves the skull without ever entering the spinal column, which makes it unique compared to the rest of the nerves in your body. It then travels throughout the neck and into the intrapleural area. It then connects to the heart and lungs to regulate and sense them, as well as to the ear. You then have your nerve travel into the epiglottis and the pharynx as it travels down into the neck and vocal folds. It is only at that point that it then ventures elsewhere throughout the body.

At this point, it wanders further, going down to the guts. It connects to the smooth muscles within the gastrointestinal and respiratory tracts to control them. This connection is what allows for the gut-brain axis—the communication between your gut and your brain, as the name implies.

All of this happens with many different functions. The nerve needs to do all sorts of different functionalities to ensure that you are able to run your body properly. Without the vagus nerve, or when the vagus nerve is faulty in some way, you start to run into all sorts of problems, ranging from mental health issues, such as anxiety or depression, or even physical problems related to the immune system. When you cannot regulate out your vagus nerve, you cannot ensure that your body works well.

We have been watching the vagus nerve closely in modern science. It has been found that you can stimulate the vagus nerve when it does not work properly, and in doing so, you ensure that you are able to keep it functioning. You effectively shock it into working to allow for regulation of symptoms related to inflammatory diseases, treatment-resistant depression, and many others as well. It has even been found to help manage epilepsy. We will be going into detail about this later, but for now, keep in mind that you can individually stimulate the vagus nerve to tap into its power.

## Cranial Nerves

Your vagus nerve is a cranial nerve—one of twelve pairs of nerve sets that are a direct line of communication from the body to the brain. Aside from this handful of nerve pairs, the rest of your body is only able to connect to the brain through the spine. This is why a severance of the spine can lead to paralysis—all of that feedback to your body is through the spinal column and the nerves that make up the spinal cord, and when that gets damaged, you run into a problem of no longer having a means of communication from the brain to the body.

The cranial nerves, however, do not require this. They bypass the spinal cord altogether and run throughout the body to serve their functions. For the most part, these nerves are tied to senses—they connect the various sensory organs to the brain and allow you to process information such as sight, smell, taste, and other sensory stimuli. This refers to their sensory functions—they are afferent and bring the information straight to the brain. However, cranial nerves also allow for the creation of motor functions. These allow for movement to occur within the areas that are sensing something. You may be able to move your eyes to track something that is moving, for example, or move your tongue.

The vagus nerve is just one of these pairs of nerves—it is referred to commonly as the 10th cranial nerve, and it is quite important. While all of your cranial nerves are important to varying degrees, what is important to note is that the vagus nerve is one of the more complex. It is particularly important due to being that lifeline of communication between the body and the brain. Without this connection and communication, you run the risk of not being able to properly function your body. We will primarily be focusing on this particular nerve.

## Anatomy of the Vagus Nerve

The vagus nerve can primarily be divided into two different portions to understand it: The dorsal vagal complex and the ventral vagal complex. We will be looking at how this nerve goes through the body and allows for the visceral experiences of the body. They are primarily responsible for stress responses within mammals. Some parts are more primitive that will lead you to freeze, such as playing dead when you are being pursued by something. Other functions are more evolved and more responsible for social settings. We will be looking at it all when considering how this nerve functions. In looking at these two branches of the vagus nerve, you can begin to understand how the body responds to stress and why you do what you do. Usually, the primitive systems are less prioritized than the others—they are there to be activated as a sort of last-ditch effort to keep you alive. After all, they are primitive for a reason—you have evolved new methods that are supposed to be better for you in general.

**Dorsal vagal complex**

The dorsal branch begins at the dorsal motor nucleus and is typically recognized to be the older of the two branches. It is primarily unmyelinated, referring to the fact that it does not have a myelin sheath in the way that most of your neurons do. This myelination is what allows for nerves to fire at a quicker rate than they otherwise would. Most vertebrates have this particular nerve, regardless if they are mammals or reptiles—it allows for the basic freeze response that you would see when you scare an animal. Frogs and lizards, when threatened, typically freeze. This allows for a conservation of the energy within the metabolism so it can be used if necessary.

In general, this will allow for control of the visceral organs that exist beneath the diaphragm, which is primarily the digestive tract. It manages the ability to digest food, as well as the freezing that you may see when under stress. When you see a person freeze, there is a good chance that they are using their dorsal vagal complex to respond to the stress in their life at that particular moment.

**Ventral vagal complex**

Over time, however, mammals have had plenty of time to develop this part of the brain. The vagus nerve took time and evolution to grow into the nerve that you know today. This came with further functionality and methods of handling stressors around you, such as being able to act when exposed to fear.

In particular, the ventral vagal complex is known as the smart vagus in contrast to the dorsal vagal complex's reputation as the vegetative vagus. This is where you are going to start seeing myelination on the nerves, insulating them and helping them to fire quicker than the other areas. The ventral vagal complex begins to activate sympathetic regulation from this area—it can use the parasympathetic response to take away power from the sympathetic fight or flight response, for example.

The behaviors that will primarily be attributed to this area of the brain include social communication and attempts at self-soothing.

Essentially, this complex is capable of regulating and inhibiting or disinhibiting defensive methods that your body uses. It does more than this as well; however—it controls areas such as your controlling the visceral organs above the diaphragm, such as the heart and lungs, as well as impacting the esophagus, bronchi, pharynx, and the larynx. This allows for the vagus nerve to be able to but a sort of limiting factor over the heart's pace at any given point of time. It keeps your heart from beating far quicker than it otherwise would. Your resting heart rate, for example, is the product of your vagus nerve activating and controlling your heart. It slows it down because there is no real reason for the heart to be pumping at full speed when there is no stress around you.

**Purpose of the Vagus Nerve**

This all happens for very specific reasons—your body has this nerve to regulate many different systems. Let's take a look at some of the primary capabilities of the vagus nerve:

• It grants sensory functionality: The vagus nerve specifically allows for certain areas of the body to transmit sensory information. In particular, data about the functionality of your heart, lungs, and digestive tract all go through the vagus nerve. It allows for your body to know how to regulate your breathing, your heart rate, and the digestion of food, allowing it to control when to propel food from the stomach into the intestines for further digestion.

• It allows for special sensory functions: Special sensory functions are those that are specifically related to your five senses of sight, smell, touch, hearing, and taste. In particular, the vagus nerve innervates an area of the tongue that is responsible for taste at the base of the tongue.

• It allows for motor functions to occur: The vagus nerve also controls your movements in many different areas. Have you ever thought about how much goes into ensuring that you are

160

able to swallow food, for example? Swallowing requires the activation of many different muscles throughout the mouth and neck, and yet we do it effortlessly thanks to the vagus nerve. It regulates these movements that you need to use to eat and speak.

•     It regulates your parasympathetic nervous system: Your parasympathetic nervous system is a crucial part of your autonomic functionality. It allows you to cope with the stressors in your environment. In particular, the parasympathetic nervous system is meant to sort of shut off the fight, flight, and freeze response that your body is likely to have when you engage with something that is a cause of concern for you.

# Chapter 17 : The Polyvagal Theory

The Polyvagal Theory splits the autonomic nervous system into three branches. These branches have evolved considerably from primitive animals and are now in their most developed stage in us humans. When we understand these branches, we are able to get a deeper insight into how we are able to assess stressful situations and react to them accordingly.

## The Complexity of Emotions

We often like to consider our emotions as something ethereal, mysterious, and complex. We cannot easily identify the way they work.

But in reality, our emotions are fairly simple mechanisms. They are our reactions to certain stimuli, whether those stimuli are external or internal. An example of an external stimulus is when someone says something to you, and you display an emotion in response. On the other hand, an example of an internal stimulus is where you realize that you have an upset stomach and you begin to display emotions in response to that.

Normally, our nervous system is always functioning in the background. It is subtly controlling our bodily functions and regulating our stress responses so that we can focus on other things, such as ordering our favorite drink at the cafe, enjoying a nice TV show, or having a wonderful conversation with someone. In other words, the nervous system is constantly influencing our emotions.

When it comes to our emotional response towards stressful situations, the Polyvagal Theory concludes that our primal need to stay alive is more important to our body than any other form of thought. That is why we often lose track of rational behavior and our ability to maintain our emotions when are faced with stressful situations. Our nervous system takes over rational thought and begins to go through a series of steps. Each step represents one of the three branches of the autonomic nervous system.

This is because it might get a little confusing if we suddenly dive into the complexities of the three branches. Let's begin by getting to know more about how our nervous system reacts to stressful scenarios.

### The Lion and the Deer

One of the best ways to understand how we handle stress is to examine animals. This is because animals display the simplest form of fight-or-flight responses that we exhibit.

If you have ever watched an Animal Planet documentary on lions and the way they stalk their prey, then you might be aware of what usually happens. The documentary often starts with a group of deer grazing or drinking water by a small pond.

Suddenly, one of them looks up, as though it sensed something that the others didn't. The deer's sympathetic nervous system has been activated, sending the necessary chemicals throughout its body to focus its senses. Now the entire group is hyper-alert. Their ears twitch, trying to catch any sounds that are out of the ordinary. Their heads are moving constantly, as though they want to make sure that they get visual confirmation of the threat to the environment.

After a while, the lion springs into the action. It begins the chase as it runs towards the group. It has so many targets to choose from, so right now its main priority is to get to the group as soon as possible. One particular deer is singled out. When the deer realizes that it is the target of the hunt, it begins to run. Earlier, its sympathetic nervous system was on alert mode. Now it realizes that the threat is real and that it is in danger.

Eventually, the deer is caught. The lion begins to drag it towards its cubs. At this point, the deer's parasympathetic system kicks in and the deer goes limp. It realizes that it has been caught and there is no point in worrying about the situation. Rather, it chooses to play dead to throw the lion's attention off course.

When the lion brings the deer back to its cubs, they play with the animal before eating it. If the lion becomes distracted, then the sympathetic system of the deer starts up again. The deer lifts itself up, as though it has returned from the dead and sprints away to safety.

## Immobilization

When humans used to live in caves, they were always on the lookout for predators. Their lives depended on the fact that they were alert. If they lost their focus for even a few brief moments, they could be on the menu of a hungry predator. But their sense of alertness was not just reserved for beasts. They used their heightened awareness to keep track of their environment so that they didn't accidentally step on venomous plants or fail to recognize changes in weather to flee from an incoming storm. When their senses were on high alert, they would freeze to better assess the threat. They would try and pick out noises, check for scents, and look out for anything out of the ordinary in the environment.

This is what happens during the first stage of a stress response.

The immobilization is the most basic step. The vagus nerve realizes that there is a threat in the environment and your dorsal vagus takes over, immobilizing you completely to help you gauge the threat. It feels as though your sympathetic nervous system is not allowed to increase the fight-or-flight response threat levels just yet. Not until you can properly understand what is going on.

There is another purpose for the dorsal vagus to immobilize you. To understand this purpose, it is first important to look into a part of the brain that helps greatly in our fight-or-flight response: The hypothalamus.

165

## The Hypothalamus

The hypothalamus is a fairly small region in the brain that is located at its base. Despite its size, however, the hypothalamus plays an important role in numerous functions such as:

• Releasing hormones

• Maintaining daily physiological cycles

• Regulating emotional responses

• Controlling appetite

• Managing sexual behavior

• Regulating body temperature.

It is the hypothalamus that sends a signal to the sympathetic nervous system that there is a threat in the environment. The hypothalamus then releases numerous hormones, the most important of which is the hormone cortisol. When your body releases cortisol, it increases the heart rate to supply your body with the required amount of blood to help you feel the situation, should you choose to do so. At the same time, the hypothalamus tenses your body, getting it ready to spring into action. It helps more blood to pass into the brain, making the organ hyper-alert to process information in the environment. In short, your body is in a high state of stress.

## How Is the Dorsal Vagus Involved in This Process?

When your body becomes alert, your dorsal vagus intentionally immobilizes you so that you are better able to process the information you receive from the environment. If you are in a state of motion, you are distracted by too many actions. You have to balance your body, make sure you don't bump into objects, maintain your speed, and perform numerous calculations to move properly. When your brain handles these calculations, it is too overwhelmed to notice what is happening around you. However, if you were standing still, then your brain is only focused on one task; finding out the source of the threat.

However, there is another reason why you freeze. When you are immobile, you are conserving as much energy as possible. If you simply start moving, then you conserve energy, making you tired for no reason. To make sure you have sufficient energy to use if you decide to start running, the dorsal vagus helps you recognize the threat. If there is no threat, then it was just a false alarm and your body begins to relax. Your energy is conserved. However, if there is a threat, then energy is diverted to the most essential parts of your body to aid your flight.

## Mobilization

And now, we enter the next phase of the fight-or-flight reaction. Remember that if you perceived that there was no threat in the environment, then you won't reach this stage. You simply return to a relaxed state and go back to doing what you were originally engaged in.

However, when your brain realizes that there is indeed a threat in the environment, then your body is ready to react. You either decide to take a stand against the threat or you decide to flee from the threat. Each reaction is based on millions of calculations performed by your brain at the same time.

But what if things are not so simple? Could there be a situation where we are unable to process information properly? As a matter of fact, there is.

**There Is Nothing Normal About Normalcy Bias**

Imagine this scenario. You are on a Boeing 747 airplane as it is just about to approach the runway for landing. The landing gear has been deployed and you hear and feel the deep rumble as the tires make contact with the ground. The 747 taxies along the runway before slowing down. Now begins the tedious process of slowly taxiing towards the designated arrival gates for the plane. You cannot wait for the plane to stop. You see hundreds of passengers around you taking out their cellphones, talking to their family members, checking their belongings, and simply performing actions to prepare themselves for the exit procedures.

Without warning, a shockwave ripples through the airplane. Heat and pressure tear into your flesh. You hear a loud noise that almost sounds like two trains have collided with each other. The noise is deafening, causing your eardrums to take in severe damage. An explosion follows this noise, steams of flames trying to get into every space and crevice in the plane. You see fire above your head and beneath your feet.

Now, try to ask yourself this question: If you find yourself in such a scenario, what would you do? You might be thinking that you would immediately start taking action, trying to look for water or maybe try and save people. Or perhaps you might think that your first reaction would be to panic and try and escape the inferno. Or you could even start screaming on top of your voice in sheer panic.

However, there is another possibility, one that is strange and at odds with rational behavior.

The above scenario did happen. In 1977, two airplanes crashed into each other while one was still taxiing along the runway. A KLM flight asked to be cleared for takeoff. At the time, visibility was extremely low due to thick fog covering the airport. The control tower made a quick decision; they gave a go-ahead signal for the KLM flight, not realizing that a Pan Am aircraft was still taxiing along the same runway. The result was that the KLM crashed into the Pan Am flight at 160 miles an hour as it was taking off. This caused the KLM flight to bounce off the Pan Am aircraft, lose control, and then eventually crash in a fiery explosion. Rescue teams could see the glow of flames through the fog and headed in the direction, completely ignoring the Pan

Am aircraft, which at that moment was slowly becoming engulfed in flames.

When paramedics and rescue teams eventually reached them, they were able to rescue a few passengers but mentioned something odd when describing the scene much later. According to them, the passengers had a full two minutes to remove their seatbelts and jump out of the huge hole that had appeared on one side of the aircraft. During that time, several dozen people simply failed to take action. They were unable to break free of their paralysis. Here is the kicker: These people were not in a state of shock.

Psychologists studying this behavior discovered something completely strange about people who experience disasters. When they are witnessing the situation unfold, their brains become so overwhelmed with ambiguous information that they just don't do anything at all. They simply become immobile and refuse to do anything. Their brain just seems to shut down.

In many cases, you become unable to deal with the copious amount of stress and anxiety. Your brain cannot simply handle the information that it is receiving. In such cases, your brain knows that you are not in any danger when things are safe and expected. Your brain then engages in a self-soothing behavior, convincing itself that everything is fine. It begins to engage in normal habits because the more it believes that things are normal, the more it can manage your stress and anxiety levels.

170

This is what normalcy bias is. It is a state of mind where your brain is attempting to make you believe that everything is okay.

During a fight-or-flight response, you evaluate the situation and when you perceive a threat, you immediately begin to take action. You only return to a state of normalcy when the threat has passed or you have dealt with it.

Remember how we explained that the dorsal vagus relaxes you to a point where you become immobile? When your brain has entered into a state of normalcy bias, then there is a jumble of information. Your dorsal vagus tries to calm the rising stress and anxiety in your body. But when you enter the immobilization stage, the information that you receive is too much for your brain to handle. It cannot sift through the information to decide what is valuable and what should be discarded for the moment.

Instead of choosing to go through all the information at its disposal, it decides to bring you to a normal state. Your brain does this because it believes that if you reach a state of normalcy, then it can go through the information in a reasonable, calmer state. Your anxieties won't get in the way of the brain's evaluation and investigative process.

Image 4: In some cases, people who are affected by normalcy bias sit down and make themselves comfortable. They simply want to make themselves feel normal.

**Training Fight-or-Flight**

Now, you might wonder how it is that police officers and firemen don't enter normalcy bias. After all, don't they go through stressful situations on a daily basis?

Here is something you should know about your brain; it does not do anything it is not aware of. In other words, the way it forms ideas and conclusions are based on information that it already has. Police officers and firefighters are trained every day to handle stressful situations. Firemen use daily practice drills to train themselves into getting into action as quickly as possible after they hear the emergency alarm go off. They do this so many times that their brains form a habit to get them into action even before they have fully processed the crisis they are about to deal with. This allows their brain to forget thinking about getting prepared since that is performed automatically by the firemen. The brain's computing power is then reserved for other information, thus preventing it from becoming overwhelmed.

Have you ever been in a situation where you are walking outside, and someone falls to the ground? One or two people might rush to the person to help while others may continue walking as though nothing has happened? This too is a result of the normalcy bias. The fight-or-flight instincts kick in because people are wondering why someone would fall. Is there a larger threat that they should be aware of? The dorsal vagus sends them into a sudden state of relaxation. However, at this point, other social cues take over.

Why did the person fall? Is the person hurt? Should someone help the person get up? Should I help the person get up? But wouldn't that be embarrassing? What if I try to help the person and slip myself? What if I am about to reach the person but someone else comes there faster, making me feel so stupid in the middle of the street? Perhaps I could stop and take a look?

As you can see, the brain is already overloaded with information and simply forces a normalcy bias onto you. You could say that it is your brain's way of saying, "Could you please shut up? I'm trying to focus here!"

If you would like to override such behaviors, then you need to first examine yourself. Try to train yourself or your thoughts to react to situations in a particular way. Let's take the above example. You can train yourself to reach out to someone when they fall. However, you cannot train yourself daily as firemen do. After all, it's not every day you come across a person falling down randomly on the street. In such situations, you can train your mind instead. Try to think about all the reasons that prevent you from helping someone in need. Then slowly answer them while instilling the idea in your mind that helping others is okay, even if it leads to an embarrassing situation.

# Chapter 18 : The Polyvagal Theory And Emotional Regulation

Along with stress management comes the desperate need for emotional regulation. We all have emotions that are meant to guide us—we have discussed this. However, what happens when your emotions are leading you down the wrong path? What happens when you realize that your response to the stress that you are feeling is incredibly unhealthy or you see how what you are doing is going to be a problem at the end of the day? When you realize that your emotional regulation system is not functioning properly, you are going to realize that you need to do some serious work on yourself.

We need to be able to regulate our emotions—it is critical when it comes to dealing with people. If everyone responded to situations based on their emotions, we would find that people would be far angrier on a far more regular basis, and you would not be able to avoid very serious repercussions. You must be able to regulate your emotions if you want to have good relationships with other people. You must be able to recognize what you are doing and how what you are doing could facilitate a good or a bad relationship with someone else if you wish to have any meaningful relationships with other people.

Within this chapter, we are going to look at emotional regulation in depth. We will discuss why it is so important and how you can know if you are struggling with it. When you can identify this, you can then begin to treat the problems that you are suffering from. You will be able to stop yourself before you ruin your relationships everywhere that you go, and when you can do that, you will find that you are far happier. Just the act of learning how to be more regulated can help you feel more regulated itself.

## What is Emotional Regulation?

Emotional regulation is something that, as an adult reading this book, you are expected to be able to manage on your own without any effort. However, it is not that simple. People struggle with emotional regulation just because emotions themselves are designed to be motivational. They are designed to drive you toward very specific actions and yet, so often, those emotional tendencies that you have and that you want to act upon are entirely misguided in the first place. You may desperately want to go ahead and yell because you are angry, but at the end of the day, yelling will not solve the problem. Yelling will not help the other person listen better. Yelling will not lead to some solution that no one saw beforehand.

Emotional regulation is difficult—it is being able to superimpose what is socially acceptable atop the emotions that you are already happening. It is being able to stop yourself, say that screaming sounds great, but you know that it will not help, and

175

then deciding to do something else. Sure, screaming would have felt great in the moment. Screaming would have helped you to release that tension, but at what cost? At what point is it better to attempt to do something entirely different to succeed? When you are able to socially manage yourself better, you usually know how to regulate your emotions, at least to some degree. You would have to—if you want to succeed in your relationships, you cannot always act on that first feeling that you feel. You cannot always choose to follow that impulse blindly because, most of the time, it will not help you. Most of the time, following that impulse is going to be wrong to some degree and choosing to do so can hurt you.

Essentially, then, emotional regulation is your ability to avoid emotional explosions on other people while still managing yourself and your expectations for the relationships that you are in. Even though emotions are designed to motivate you into actions, you can learn to overcome that. You can learn to resist that desire to give in to those emotional impulses. You can learn to think rationally and make decisions that you know are going to help you in life. It is only when you master this skill that you can truly have a healthy social engagement system that you desire.

## Struggling With Emotional Regulation

Unfortunately, despite being such a desired skill, emotional regulation is quite fleeting. It is incredibly difficult in times of great emotion to have the wherewithal to stop yourself, remind yourself that what you are doing is not the right choice at that particular moment, and then redirect yourself. This requires you to develop not only a great deal of emotional self-awareness, but also a great degree of emotional self-control, and that is something that can be just as rare.

When you struggle with your emotional regulation, you oftentimes end up behaving in ways that disrupt those around you. They are oftentimes inappropriate, and even though your emotions are what they are, your actions are not treated as kindly. People will generally be okay with you being angry during a meeting, so long as you do not start throwing books, mugs, and anything else that you can get your hands on at people's heads. So long as you are able to keep yourself under control, you are entitled to your emotions, just like everyone else is. However, that emotional control is the defining factor there. You need to be able to engage in emotional control or you will fail in life. You will struggle to make good relationships with other people. You will struggle to make good decisions. You will be unable to manage yourself well. You may find that you are impulsive or irrational.

Let's go over some of the signs of being unable to control your emotions:

•      You are regularly overwhelmed by your emotions in many contexts

- You are afraid to express the emotions that you do have, either due to not trusting them, being ashamed of them, or being unsure how people will treat your emotions in the first place

- You are angry often, but you never know why you are, despite trying to figure out the reason

- You feel like you have no control or like you are at the utter mercy of your emotions

- You feel like you are entirely unaware of why you feel the way that you feel at any given point in time

- You find that you are happier using drugs or alcohol to sort of avoid facing your negative emotions

Sometimes, the symptoms can be more irregular or problematic. Sometimes, if you struggle to manage your emotions, you may find that you struggle with suicidal tendencies or feel like you want to self-harm. This is not something that you should be dealing with on your own, and you should speak to a doctor if you find that you do struggle with thoughts of suicide or self-harm. You do not have to live this way and a doctor can help you.

## Emotional Regulation and the Polyvagal Theory

Emotional regulation, so far, has been one of the primary purposes of this book. It is being able to manage yourself and your feelings on the regular, and that means that you are oftentimes going to be cycling through the various activations of the vagus nerve. Sometimes, you will be feeling happier and that is a good thing—you are probably firmly feeling that feeling of connection, resting, and digesting. That means that all is right in your world. Other times, you are going to be oscillating strongly between feelings of anxiety, depression, or other feelings that may be problematic for you. You may feel like you want to hurt or fight someone when you are angry thanks to that fight response, or when you get stressed, you may entirely shut down, due to your freeze response.

Essentially, then, you are going to want to be able to engage in your emotional regulation on the regular. You are going to need to master the art of shifting back to that calming center within yourself to avoid causing problems in your life that can just make things worse. Think about it—if you are already angry and decide to hit someone else, any problem that you had before is now worse. You will most likely then be dealing with someone who wants to press charges, for example—you will be involved in the courts and struggling to navigate a situation that just got a whole lot more complicated.

If you cannot engage in this sort of emotional self-regulation that you need, you are going to struggle. You are going to fail. You are going to flounder and make the situation worse more often than not. When you can self-regulate, you can remind yourself to stop and take that deep breath. You can return to that calm state so you can make an informed decision, so you know that at the end of the day, you have made the right one.

## Managing Emotional Regulation With Vagal Activation

Much like with managing stress, when you need to be able to emotionally regulate yourself, you are going to need to trigger the activation of your social engagement system. You need to get to that point to aid you in making the decisions that are right for you. Stop and think about things this way—when you can stop yourself and activate that part of your mind that wants to interact in a meaningful manner, you are going to recognize that what you are doing is just causing more harm than good. You will be able to trigger that sort of realization that will guide you—you will be able to use that realization alone to remind yourself to stop, so you do not cause further problems.

The fact that you will naturally want that relationship to be salvaged, no matter how angry that you are in the moment, will be your motivator. You will be able to keep yourself focused and centered. You will be able to see the value in forcing yourself to act against nature, and in doing so, you will better facilitate those relationships.

# Chapter 19 : How Mindfulness Meditation Stimulates Your Vagus Nerve

Let's talk about mindfulness meditation, and how it can stimulate your vagus nerve.

One of the best ways to stimulate your vagus nerve is through meditation. Why is that? That's because there is a correlation between meditation and the vagus nerve. They both offer very similar physical and psychological benefits to your health.

The vagus nerve helps reduce symptoms of depression, which is what mindfulness meditation can do as well. When done correctly, mindfulness meditation can help lower inflammation within the body, and improve the ability of the brain to manage anxiety and stress.

## Why Meditation?

Non-invasive procedures, like meditation, that stimulate the vagus nerve are great for depression. Mindfulness meditation is one of the best ways to stimulate your vagus nerve, and it's a focal part of holistic medicine. Those who suffer from depression will sometimes notice that when the vagus nerve is stimulated, their depression improves. When you practice mindfulness meditation, you stimulate your vagus nerve, relax the body, and feel amazing.

The best part about mindfulness meditation is that it's inexpensive, meaning it's free, and is not invasive. When you practice mindfulness meditation, you can do it all on your own in a quiet place, free of any people. Meditate on your actions. You can even do this throughout the day, walking around and meditating on a few different aspects of life.

This is a simple way to help stimulate the vagus nerve. After all, when your attention is focused on being mindful and breathing correctly, you'll be much happier over time. Mindfulness meditation also greatly helps with keeping your body grounded and calm.

## What Is Mindfulness?

What is mindfulness? Mindfulness refers to the awareness of your surroundings, the people around you, your environment, etc. Throughout life, we simply don't pay attention to what others do or the things we see. We walk around almost as if we're in a fog, and we don't pay much attention to the actions we undertake. That's why, when we start to become mindful, we'll notice immediately the things we didn't before. This can be a rude awakening in a sense, but it's a wonderful way to stimulate the vagus nerve, simply because you're paying attention to your actions and surroundings.

Mindfulness helps with cognitive thinking, improving attention and intention, but along with that, relaxing the body in a sense that's natural. If you're feeling stressed, it might be helpful to practice mindfulness meditation. It will help to reduce instances of stress, depression, and the likes. If you are treatment-resistant, you'll notice that this type of natural treatment can help stimulate the neurotransmitters in the body, which in turn, will help wake up your vagus nerve.

**The Power Of Mindfulness Meditation**

Mindfulness meditation helps improve the connections in your brain and body.

When the body doesn't have the right connections in place, or is struggling with these connections, inflammations within the body will increase, and as a result you will suffer from the damages of free radicals, inflammation, and the likes. But, with mindfulness meditation, you can learn to relax the body. You will then be able to naturally stimulate neurotransmitters, reducing inflammation in place too. If you notice that you're struggling with controlling the way your body acts and completes various activities, this might be the answer you're looking for. If you feel like you have no control over yourself and your body, this can be a natural way to reduce the stressors at hand, improving your ability to connect with the different parts of your body. You'll learn to have better control of yourself, your body, and of course, your mind too.

Mindfulness is super easy to start as well, and while it might be slow-going when it comes to changes, it does help with feeling relaxed, and with improving your ability to stimulate the vagus nerve naturally.

Doing this right before bed is a good way to stimulate the vagus nerve, which will aid with breathing, heart rate, and digestion. You'll be able to reduce the instances of pain, inflammation, headaches, and more with the power of mindfulness.

A little goes a long way when it comes to mindfulness. You don't need to sit there for hours on end; simply meditating for 15-30 minutes each day will properly stimulate the vagus nerve.

**How To Practice Mindfulness Meditation**

So, how do you practice mindfulness meditation? That answer is quite easy.

To start, what you'll want to do is sit down in a place that's quiet where you can't be disturbed. Take a moment to place your attention on your body, and become more mindful of it. Focus your attention on your body. Do you notice anything strange going on with your body when you focus your attention on it? Chances are, you might realize that you're not as aware of your body as you thought you were. That is perfectly fine. Many people come to this realization the first time they practice mindful meditation.

You can also do this while walking around. Take a walk around the block, around the park, or even around the office. Pay attention to how you physically feel, how you are breathing, your heart rate, and everything else. You'll notice that as you do this, your heart rate will slow down over time, which will help you to feel relaxed. As you do this, start to pay mind to your surroundings, the visuals you possess. You'll start to notice over time that being mindful and aware is easy.

If you notice stress or intrusive thoughts coming in, acknowledge them, but don't let them adversely affect you. Instead, take the time to properly acknowledge them, so that they're not affecting you in the ways that they would in the past. As you continue, you'll notice your mental focus is improving. You will be able to see and think more clearly.

For most people, mindfulness meditation wakes you up, unlocks your potential, and the abilities that you have. Even doing this with your daily activities, such as becoming mindful of how you brush your teeth, how you brush every little tooth, the feeling of your gums as you floss them, and also how your teeth feel afterward, can wake you up. Taking a shower, feeling the water against your body, your feet against the shower tiles, and how you feel when the water hits you is a great way to practice mindfulness.

**Mindfulness When Stressed**

One way to activate the vagus nerve, is to practice mindfulness when you're stressed out. Let's say that you have a lot of work going on, or maybe you're stressed about school or your family, whatever it may be. In such cases, take a deep breath in, and for a moment, focus on three things that innervate the mind and put your full attention on those three things. It might be easier to do it one by one.

Think about some of the different things that are happening around you. If you're at the office, think about the sounds you hear, the visuals you see, maybe even the scents you smell. Think about the placement of your body.

At the same time, practice deep breathing. Deep breathing while practicing mindfulness allows you to focus on your body's energy.

Do you notice yourself feeling more relaxed? Do you feel better? If the answer is yes, then go back to whatever you were doing during the day, but remain mindful. Don't just disregard all that you just did.

If you don't feel relaxed just yet, continue to practice mindfulness. Instead of falling into the trap of your unwanted thoughts, think about something important that's currently present in your life.

**Can You Combine Meditation And Mindfulness?**

Of course! That's the whole purpose of this chapter. Mindfulness meditation is one of the best ways to relax your body all while stimulating the vagus nerve. It's totally up to you whether you choose to meditate or be mindful. You can even combine the two. Naturally, both will converge without you possibly even being aware of it.

I like to practice mindfulness meditation when I'm in the car. I'll sit there, and become mindful of everything. The touch of the steering wheel, the seat belt running across my body, the texture of my seat, the smells inside my car. I focus on my breathing, taking deep breaths in and out, all while remaining present.

I gently push out any thoughts that come into my mind about the workday, any stress of life, etc.

Try it for yourself and see what happens. I can guarantee that you will notice a huge difference in how you feel immediately.

Yoga And How It Stimulates Your Vagus Nerve

Did you know you could use yoga to stimulate the vagus nerve? That's right, it can be done, and it can play a critical role in the health of your vagus nerve. Yoga practices that stimulate these areas will drastically change your vagal tone. Certain yoga practices are better than others, as they all serve different purposes. In this chapter, we'll highlight what positions are best to try and how they stimulate your vagus nerve.

## Vagus Nerve Yoga And How It Helps

Vagus nerve yoga isn't just for the vagus nerve, but it's for overall general stress reduction. So, even if your vagus nerve isn't completely out of sorts, it will change your life.

Yoga combines slow movements of the body, utilization of your breath, mindfulness, use of your senses, and remaining in the present moment. As you practice yoga, you become more mindful of your body and how you are using it. You also become mindful of how you breathe in and out. Yoga is an excellent practice to not only relax your body but become grounded too. It's very similar to meditation, only it involves more movement.

I like to practice yoga after a long day, or after a chaotic at the office to relax my body and reduce any stress. It's also a great way to help stimulate the vagus nerve and I can feel the effects of it instantly.

While we've touched upon diaphragmatic breathing and its importance, below we'll discuss several yoga techniques you can follow to stimulate your vagus nerve.

## The Half-Smile

First, is the half-smile. This might seem silly, but it stimulates your vagus nerve and changes your mental state completely. The concept behind this is simple. Relax your facial muscles. Then, take your hands and pull on your lips in an upward motion, creating a half-smile. This engages the social nervous system, which is an evolved branch of your vagus nerve. After you've pulled your lips into a half-smile, imagine the jaw softening and the feeling of relaxation spreading all through your face, head, and down your shoulders, all the way to your extremities. This technique will subtly change the quality of your emotions and thoughts.

## Open Your Heart

The next technique requires you to open your heart. This is a stimulation of the vagus nerve that involves opening your chest and throat, and it helps create a more open feeling to your body. What you need to do is you bring your hands directly to your chest, and from there, inhale as you expand your hands from your chest, slowly open up your elbows, and then lifting your chin. Take deep breaths as you move with this, focusing on the inhalation in the pattern of breathing, so that it's stimulating and uplifting. From there, expand your chest so that your heart is open.

This is a simple stretch, and is a wonderful and simple activity that will help with your ability to open up, and understand yourself more. This is also a great pose if you have a lot of pent up energy. The stress of a long day, the trouble of the events all around you, opening your heart can do you some good, and it can help with improving how you approach the world around you. It will enable you to relax the body and feel mentally stronger and healthier than ever before.

## The Power Of Yoga Stretching

Do you feel tired and unmotivated when you wake up in the morning? Have you ever woken up and stretched first thing? This is something you can do whenever you're feeling tired in the morning, or during the day to help stimulate your mind and body.

The warrior pose is one of the best yoga poses. Find a space where you can get into this pose. Get into a lunge stance, and turn your torso to the side. Stretch your arms out with your palms facing downward. Notice the connection of your feet to the ground, remaining grounded and energized. Breathe rhythmically, in and out. Connect with the sensations that you feel within your body. This is a great pose to help you not only stretch but also feel connected and grounded.

Take about 5-10 minutes every day to do simple stretches. As you stretch, visualize everything slowly coming apart, your body slowly growing with each passing moment. Think about your blood flowing through every part of your body. Think about it nourishing your body with all that it needs. Focus on your breathing and think about the air flowing through your body also, oxygenating all of it.

## Release The Belly

Release the belly is another great pose, and it's encouraged simply because your vagus nerve has a connection to the abdominal cavity. What you will want to do is get on the ground into a table position with your hands under the shoulders and knees beneath your hips. You can put a blanket underneath your hands and knees if the ground is not soft. As you inhale, lift your head and your hips and lower your belly to the floor. When you exhale, you should lower your hips and head, and then lift the spine. Move with your breath, moving as many times as you can, creating a massage that's gentle to the belly, and the spine of the body as well. This is good for fully releasing any tension within the body, making it easier for you to relax, and to help you with improving your wellness and generalized health as well.

Many of us hold tension in our stomachs. We might not realize it, but anxiety, trouble with bowel movements and stress may exist because you're holding tension within the belly. As you release it, focus on letting out all of that tension. Doing this after a long day does wonders for improving your wellness. By releasing it, you can relax, feel more comfortable, and stimulate your vagus nerve too.

**Loving-Kindness Meditation**

Do you ever think about wishing kindness to others and the world? We oftentimes are so focused on ourselves that we don't think about the kindness we can provide to others. Through loving-kindness meditation, we can focus that energy outwards, and in turn, feel better inside. Even when things are tough, providing love and kindness will help bring you more joy and happiness.

If you're not already practicing loving-kindness yoga, this is a great one to try. When you inhale, extend your hands out, and focus on the love that's being pushed inside of you by your hands. As you exhale, move your arms very slowly, and imagine all of the love going out in each direction. You can also do this by imagining that you're pushing out any stresses that are inside of you. Think about those who are going through something similar. Think about how you can evoke a sense of kindness and compassion to the other individual, and how the feeling of compassion feels within you. From there, wish that same feeling for yourself, and see if you can extend kindness and compassion to yourself. This practice is therapeutic and is especially great for vagus nerve stimulation.

## Yoga Nidra: What It Is And How it Helps

Finally, there's yoga nidra. This is a restorative yoga practice that will help calm your nervous system. This is a yoga sleep that is both meditative and relaxing. This is one of the best types of practices since it's an antidote and solution to the stress you may be experiencing in your life. It allows you to restore your body and mind through unlocking and touching on the parasympathetic nervous system.

Find a position on the floor that's comfortable. You can choose to sit on a blanket or mat. Start to build awareness of your breath. The body will naturally make space for feeling. Stay seated and still for about 30 minutes. This will create a relaxing and nourishing experience.

When it comes to yoga, you'll want to try these different techniques and poses to see which ones work best for you. By practicing yoga, you create a restorative action for your body, and help keep yourself grounded. Additionally, all of these yoga poses and practices stimulate the vagus nerve, which will help with improving your life, and your ability to handle anything that gets in your way.

# Chapter 20 : Yoga Therapy And Polyvagal Theory

Yoga therapy is a recently developing, automatic correlative and integrative human services (CIH) practice. It is developing in its professionalization, acknowledgment & use with a showed responsibility to setting practice principles, instructive & accreditation norms, and elevating exploration to help its viability for different populaces and conditions.

In any case, heterogeneity of training, poor detailing principles, and absence of an extensively acknowledged comprehension of the neurophysiological systems associated with yoga treatment restrains the organizing of testable speculations and clinical applications.

Current proposed structures of yoga-put together practices center with respect to the combination of base up neurophysiological and top-down neurocognitive components. What's more, it has been suggested that phenomenology and first individual moral request can give a focal point through which yoga treatment is seen as a procedure that contributes towards eudaimonic prosperity in the experience of torment, sickness or incapacity. In this article we expand on these systems, and propose a model of yoga treatment that merges with Polyvagal Theory (PVT).

PVT joins the development of the autonomic sensory system to the rise of prosocial practices and sets that the neural stages supporting social conduct are engaged with looking after wellbeing, development and reclamation. This logical model which associates neurophysiological examples of autonomic guidelines and articulation of enthusiastic and social conduct is progressively used as a system for understanding human conduct, stress and disease.

In particular, we portray how PVT can be conceptualized as a neurophysiological partner to the yogic ideal of the gunas, or characteristics of nature. Like the neural stages portrayed in PVT, the gunas give the establishment from which conduct, passionate and physical traits rise. We depict how these two distinct yet closely resembling structures - one situated in neurophysiology and the other in an old intelligence convention - feature yoga treatment's advancement of physical, mental and social prosperity for self-guideline and strength. This parallel between the neural foundation of PVT and the gunas of yoga is instrumental in making a translational structure for yoga treatment to line up with its philosophical establishments. Thusly, yoga treatment can work as a particular practice instead of fitting into an outside model for its usage in inquires about and clinical settings.

Mind-body treatments, including yoga treatment, are proposed to profit wellbeing and prosperity through a reconciliation of top-down and base up forms encouraging bidirectional correspondence between the cerebrum and body. Top-down procedures, for example, the guideline of consideration and setting of expectation, have been appeared to diminish mental worry just as the hypothalamic-pituitary pivot (HPA) and thoughtful sensory system (SNS) movement, and thusly balance insusceptible capacity and irritation. Base up forms, advanced by breathing procedures and development rehearses, have been appeared to impact the musculoskeletal, cardiovascular and sensory system work and influence HPA and SNS movement with attending changes in resistant capacity and passionate prosperity.

The top-down and base up forms utilized at the top of the priority list body treatments may control autonomic, neuroendocrine, enthusiastic and conduct actuation and bolster a person's reaction to challenges. Self-guideline, a cognizant capacity to keep up the security of the framework by overseeing or modifying reactions to risk or misfortune, may diminish side effects of differing conditions, for example, peevish inside disorder, neurodegenerative conditions, interminable agony, wretchedness and PTSD through the moderation of allostatic load with a going with the move-in autonomic state have proposed such a model of top-down and base up self-administrative components of yoga for mental wellbeing.

Versatility may give another advantage of mind-body treatments as it incorporates the capacity of a person to "ricochet back" and adjust in light of affliction as well as unpleasant conditions in an opportune manner to such an extent that psychophysiological assets are rationed. High strength is related to faster cardiovascular recuperation following abstract passionate encounters, less saw pressure, more noteworthy recuperation from ailment or injury and better administration of dementia and incessant agony. Traded off versatility is connected to dysregulation of the autonomic sensory system through proportions of vagal guidelines (respiratory sinus arrhythmia. Yoga is related to both improvements in proportions of mental strength and improved vagal guidelines.

This article investigates the mix of top-down and base up forms for self-guideline and versatility through both Polyvagal Theory and yoga treatment. PVT will be portrayed in connection to contemporary understandings of interoception just as the biobehavioral hypothesis of the "preliminary set", which will be characterized later. This will help to spread out an incorporated framework see from which mind-body treatments encourage the development of physiological, enthusiastic and social qualities for the advancement of self-guideline and strength.

We will look at the union of the neural stages, depicted in PVT, with the three Gunas, a fundamental idea of the yogic way of thinking that portrays the characteristics of material nature.

Both PVT and yoga give structures to seeing how basic neural stages (PVT) and gunas (yoga) interface the development and availability between physiological, mental and conduct characteristics. By influencing the neural stage, or guna transcendence, just as one's relationship to the ceaseless moving of these neural stages, or gunas, the individual learns aptitudes for self-guideline and strength. Also, these structures share qualities that parallel each other where the neural stage mirrors the guna power and the guna prevalence mirrors the neural stage.

PVT, and other rising hypotheses, for example, neurovisceral combination, help explain associations between the frameworks of the body, the cerebrum, and the procedures of the mind offering expanded understanding into complex examples of incorporated top-down and base up forms that are natural to mind-body treatments. PVT portrays three particular neural stages in light of apparent hazard (i.e., wellbeing, peril, and life-risk) in the condition that work in a phylogenetically decided chain of command steady with the Jacksonian guideline of disintegration. PVT acquaints the idea of neuroception with depicting the subliminal recognition of wellbeing or peril in nature through base up forms including vagal afferents, tangible info identified with outside difficulties, and endocrine components that recognize and assess ecological hazard before the cognizant elaboration by higher mind focuses.

The three polyvagal neural stages, as portrayed underneath, are connected to the practices of social correspondence, guarded procedure of activation and protective immobilization:

The ventral vagal complex (VVC) gives the neural structures that intervene in the "social commitment framework". At the point when wellbeing is recognized in the interior and outside condition, the VVC gives a neural stage to help prosocial conduct and social association by connecting the neural guideline of instinctive states supporting homeostasis and reclamation to facial expressivity and the open and expressive areas of correspondence (e.g., prosodic vocalizations and upgraded capacity to tune in to voice). The engine segment of the VVC, which starts in the core ambiguous (NA) manages and organizes the muscles of the face and head with the bronchi and heart. These associations help arrange the individual towards human association and commitment in prosocial connections and give increasingly adaptable and versatile reactions to ecological difficulties including social communications

The SNS is oftentimes connected with battle/flight practices. Battle/flight practices require initiation of the SNS and are the underlying and essential guard procedures enlisted by warm-blooded creatures. This safeguard technique requires expanded metabolic yield to help activation practices. Inside PVT the enlistment of SNS in guard pursues the Jacksonian guideline of disintegration and mirrors the versatile responses of a phylogenetically requested reaction progressively in which the VVC has neglected to alleviate risk. At the point when the SNS circuit is selected, monstrous physiological changes are remembering an expansion for muscle tone, shunting of blood from the fringe, restraint of gastrointestinal capacity, an enlargement of the bronchi, increments in pulse and respiratory rate, and the arrival of catecholamines.

This assembly of physiological assets makes way for reacting to genuine or accepted peril in the earth and towards the ultimate objectives of security and endurance. At the point when the SNS turns into the predominant neural stage, the VVC impact might be repressed for activating assets for a quick activity. Though prosocial practices and social associations are related to the VVC, the SNS is related to practices and feelings, for example, dread or outrage that help to arrange to the earth for security or wellbeing.

The dorsal vagal complex (DVC) emerges from the dorsal core of the vagus (DNX) and gives the essential vagal engine filaments to organs situated beneath the stomach. This circuit is intended to adaptably react to massive peril or dread and is the crudest (i.e., developmentally most established) reaction to stretch. Initiation of the DVC in resistance brings about an uninvolved reaction portrayed by diminished muscle tone, emotional decrease of heart yield to save metabolic assets, modification in gut and bladder work utilizing reflexive poop and pee to lessen metabolic requests required by processing.

PVT sets that through these neural stages specific physiological states, mental traits, and social procedures are associated, develop, and are made open to the person. The physiological state built up by these neural stages in light of risk or security (as decided through the coordinated procedures of neuroception) takes into consideration or limits the scope of passionate and social attributes that are open to the person

A center part of PVT is that examples of physiological state, feeling and conduct are specific to each neural stage (for a point by point audit of the neurophysiological, neuroanatomical, and developmental natural bases of PVT. For instance, the neural foundation of the VVC is proposed to associate instinctive homeostasis with passionate qualities and prosocial practices that are contradictory with the neurophysiological states, enthusiastic attributes or social practices that show in the neural foundation of protective procedures found in SNS or DVC initiation. At the point when the VVC is predominant, the vagal brake is executed and pro-social practices and enthusiastic states, for example, association and love can develop.

At the point when the SNS is the essential guarded system, the NA kills the inhibitory activity of the ventral vagal pathway to the heart to empower thoughtful enactment and social and passionate procedures of assembly are bolstered. On the off chance that the DVC idleness reaction is the cautious system, the dorsal engine core is initiated as a defensive component from agony or potential demise and dynamic reaction methodologies are not accessible.

It is imperative to take note of the VVC has different qualities that empower mixed states with the SNS (e.g., play) or with the DVC (e.g., closeness). Be that as it may, in these instances of mixed states, the VVC remains effectively available and practically contains the subordinate circuits. At the point when the VVC is practically pulled back, it advances the availability of the SNS as a guard battle/flight framework. So also, the SNS practically restrains access to the DVC immobilization shutdown reaction. In this way, the significant shutdown response that may prompt demise turns out to be neurophysiologically available just when the SNS is reflexively repressed.

## Vagal Activity, Interoception, Regulation, and Resilience

Vagal movement, using ventral vagal pathways, is recommended to be intelligent of guideline and versatility of the framework where high heart vagal tone associated with increasingly versatile top-down and base up procedures, for example, consideration guideline, full of feeling preparing and adaptability of physiological frameworks to adjust and react to the earth. Vagal control has additionally been appeared to relate with differential actuation in mind locales that manage reactions to risk evaluation, interoception, feeling guideline, and the advancement of more noteworthy adaptability in light of challenge. On the other hand, the low vagal guideline has been related with maladaptive base up and top-down handling bringing about poor self-guideline, less social adaptability, discouragement, summed up uneasiness issue, and antagonistic wellbeing results remembering expanded mortality for conditions, for example, lupus, rheumatoid joint pain, and injury.

The vagus nerve is involved 80% afferent filaments and fills in as a significant conductor for interoceptive correspondence about the condition of the viscera and inside milieu to cerebrum structures. Interoception has been investigated as basic to the connecting of top-down and base up preparing and in the examination of the connections between sensations, feelings, sentiments and sympathovagal. Backing has been found for the joining of interoceptive info, feeling and a guideline of sympathovagal balance in the separate and cingulate cortices, encouraging a bound together reaction of the person to body, mind or natural (BME) wonders.

Self-guideline is proposed to be subject to the precision with which we decipher and react to interoceptive data, with more prominent exactness prompting upgraded versatility and self-guideline. Thusly, interoception is viewed as significant in torment, habit, enthusiastic guideline, and solid versatile practices including social commitment. Furthermore, interoception has been proposed as key to versatility as the precise preparation of interior substantial states advances a brisk rebuilding of homeostatic parity.

It has been suggested that mind-body treatments are a successful device for the guideline of vagal capacity, with resulting encouraging of versatile capacities including the alleviation of unfavorable impacts related with social difficulty, the decrease of allostatic load, and the assistance of self-administrative abilities and strength of the ANS crosswise over different patient populaces and conditions.

## Polyvagal Theory & Mind-Body Therapies for Regulation & Resilience

Mind-body treatments underscore the development of physical mindfulness, including both interoception and proprioception, joined with the care based characteristics of non-judgment, non-reactivity, interest, or acknowledgment to take part in a procedure of re-evaluation of improvements. While being urged to develop familiarity with BME wonders and boosts, the individual is bolstered in a procedure of re-elucidation or re-direction to such improvements so understanding may happen and flexibility, guideline, and versatility might be cultivated.

This ability to change the relationship and response to BME wonders is believed to be fundamental for self-guideline and prosperity. It has been indicated that patients using mind-body treatments for recuperating revealed both a move as far as they can tell and reaction to negative feelings and sensations just as the improvement of self-administrative aptitudes in managing torment, enthusiastic guideline and re-examination of life circumstances.

PVT offers knowledge into how figuring out how to perceive and move the hidden neural foundation of any given psychophysiological state, may legitimately influence physiology, feeling and conduct along these lines helping the individual develop versatile procedures for guideline and flexibility to profit physical, mental and social wellbeing. As mind-body treatments influence the vagal pathways they are proposed to shape methods for "working out" these neural stages to encourage self-guideline and strength of physiological capacity, feeling guideline and prosocial practices.

Ideal neural guideline of the autonomic sensory system and the related endocrine and invulnerable frameworks is encouraged through the dynamic commitment of the VVC by using explicit developments or positions, breathing works on, reciting or contemplation which influences both top-down and base up forms.

Versatility is proposed to be cultivated by both downregulating cautious states and supporting greater adaptability and flexibility in relation to different wonders of the BME to advance physiological rebuilding just as positive mental and social states. The individual can figure out how to improve the actuation of the VVC with its homeostatic effect on the living being, just as increment the office to move all through other neural stages, for example, the SNS or DVC when genuine or saw pressure is experienced.

In total, personality body practices can show the person to make the VVC increasingly open, extend the limit of resilience to other neural stages, change the relationship and reaction to SNS and DVC neural stages that happen as common vacillations of the BME, and how to turn out to be progressively talented at moving all through these neural stages. Breathing moves inside yoga regularly encourage comparable moves in the autonomic state with focalized mental and wellbeing outcomes. These practices may likewise add to our capability to encounter association past social communications or systems and to a progressively all-inclusive and unbounded feeling of unity and association.

## Summary

Polyvagal Theory founder Porges, Ph.D., will control you bit by bit through four modules of top to bottom preparing to help you adequately incorporate the transformative intensity of Polyvagal Theory and the Social Engagement System in your training. This is what's canvassed in every module:

## The Polyvagal Theory

- Principles and highlights of the Polyvagal Theory, and how to apply it in a clinical setting

- How the Polyvagal Theory can demystify a few highlights identified with pressure-related sicknesses and mental issue, for example, PTSD, chemical imbalance, melancholy, and uneasiness

- How the Social Engagement System is undermined by pressure and injury and how to reset it

- Evolutionary changes and versatile capacities in the autonomic sensory system

- Humans' reaction chain of importance to challenges

- Three neural stages that give the neurophysiological bases to social commitment, battle/flight, and shutdown practices

Social Engagement System and Psychiatric and Behavioral Disorders

- The "face-heart" association that structures a useful social commitment framework

- How our outward appearances, vocalizations, and signals are controlled by neural components that are engaged with managing our autonomic sensory system

**Perception: Detecting and Evaluating Risk**

- How our social and physical condition triggers changes in physiological state

- Understanding how versatile physiological responses may bring about maladaptive practices

- Immobilization unafraid

- Play as a neural exercise and tuning in as a neural exercise

- Fight/flight and immobilization guard methodologies

- The adaptive function of immobilization and the related clinical troubles

- How the burdens and difficulties of life mutilate social mindfulness and dislodge unconstrained social commitment practices with protective responses

## Applying the Polyvagal Theory in Clinical Settings

- Understanding sound-related hypersensitivities

- State guideline as a central element of mental issue

- Deconstructing highlights of chemical imbalance and PTSD

- Strategies to clarify disturbance and fix of advantageous guideline

- Identifying expressive gestures that upset or fix cautious response

# Conclusion

It's never easy to admit that you have a problem with stress. It's something that we all experience, and it can also be something that ruins our lives. If you are not careful, then you will start to realize that stress isn't just something that you experience, but it becomes part of who you are. The longer you go without managing stress, the harder it will be to manage these feelings when you need to the most.

Remember that it is all a mental thing at first, but if not treated, it can turn into a physical problem rather quickly. Don't let the physical side of stress take over your body. You are the one in control! Not only will stress make you experience pain in your shoulders, jaw, and other parts of your body, but it will also increase your risk for more serious health conditions, such as stroke or heart attack.

What stresses you out isn't something that is going to stress others out every time either. What calms you won't calm other people. Don't compare yourself, because we all will always have differing perspectives on what is stressful, as well as how to react to our positive and negative emotions. Sometimes you might wish you could be that chill relaxed person, but remember that not everyone is always as calm as they might seem. There's nothing wrong with you if you find that you are stressed in a situation that others are completely fine. It doesn't matter what stresses you out. The most important thing is how you react to this feeling.

Always check in with yourself and ensure that you are doing your best to calm yourself at the root first. Challenge your thoughts and question your beliefs to see where the stress might have started. Just because a thought travels through your mind doesn't mean that it is true. Sometimes, we think of what we were taught to believe first, and the second thought that comes after can be what's most important.

Keep up with research on stress and anxiety as well. There will always be new ways for you to manage your stress. Since we still have yet to completely figure out our brains, there will always be emerging science around what it is that might make our brains operate in the way that they do.

Remember that everything is temporary. Everything is going to be OK in the end. You are the one that is creating stressful thoughts in your head. Sometimes you are just going to have to sit with your discomfort and feel the stress. It will end. Panic attacks will stop, and your stressful thoughts will calm down. Nothing that you experience is going to last forever.

Others say things that might stress you out, but you will always have options for how you react to these stressors. You won't always be able to stop others from causing you harm, and there will be plenty of people that will always know how to get under your skin. Though you are powerless in this, you are entirely in control of the way that you choose to handle these situations. Look for the ways that will help alleviate your stress the best.

You are not alone in the stress that you feel. Though you might feel isolated, crazy, too emotional, and plenty of other negative feelings associated with your stress, remember that this is a common emotion. You are not wrong, broken, bad, or crazy because of the emotions that you are feeling.

Fortunately, the last few generations have figured out how we can use the vagus nerve to our benefit, and this is slowly developing its way into a full rolling therapy treatment for many people. Researchers are still to this day and minute finding new ways to use the vagus nerve to our advantage, and tweaking it in just the right way to get the full power.

What is marvelous about this life balancing technique of vagus nerve stimulation is that it doesn't have to cost you a cent. With most cases being something that you can stimulate your nerve with at home and only a few that require a vagus nerve stimulator, it can put the power into your own hands and allow for a better quality of life overall.

Can you interact with your vagus nerve to ensure that you are able to cope better with stress? Yes, you can. And if you keep an open mind and make use of the tools that have been provided to you, you will.

CPSIA information can be obtained
at www.ICGtesting.com
Printed in the USA
LVHW020030061120
670806LV00007B/200

9 781914 019494